Working with People:
A Human Relations Guide

Leslie Minor-Evans, Ph.D.

Lowell H. Lamberton, M.A., M.B.A., A.P.C.

Both of
Central Oregon Community College
and Linfield College

GLENCOE
McGraw-Hill

New York, New York   Columbus, Ohio   Woodland Hills, California   Peoria, Illinois

Library of Congress Cataloging-in-Publication Data

Minor-Evans, Leslie.
    Working with people : a human relations guide / Leslie Minor
-Evans, Lowell H. Lamberton.
        p.   cm.
    Includes index.
    ISBN 0-256-22033-6
    1. Communication in personnel management.   2. Interpersonal
relations.   I. Lamberton, Lowell H.   II. Title.
HF5549.5.C6M53   1997
658.3—dc20
                                                    96–21352

Send all inquiries to:
Glencoe/McGraw-Hill
21600 Oxnard St., Suite 500
Woodland Hills, CA 91367-4906

Printed in the United States of America.
    4 5 6   100   04

Preface

As the twenty-first century dawns, we, the authors, are becoming increasingly aware of the tremendous need for better human relations skills in the workplace—and in society as a whole. Throughout our careers in counseling, teaching, and consulting in the fields of business and psychology, we have become aware of the need for a little book such as this. This textbook is a primer that covers the areas of human relations skills needing the most attention.

The chapters are short and digestable; the concepts are easy to grasp; and the cases are readable. *Working with People: A Human Relations Guide* is based on sound management principles and research-based psychology. This book is coauthored by a specialist in management and human relations, and by a psychologist with a background in social and applied psychology. This blend presents a balance of workplace applications knowledge and psychological insight.

More than ever, effective human relations skills are crucial to business success as organizations compete and grow in today's global business environment. Employees must have the knowledge and skill to adapt to a workplace where change is a daily reality.

FEATURES OF THE GUIDE

Opening Vignettes

Each of the book's 29 chapters opens with a brief vignette that both sets the tone for the chapter and introduces the central concept to be discussed. Students will recognize the vignettes as real-life situations.

Key Terms

Although this book doesn't spend a great deal of time on the level of technical terminology, terms inevitably must be introduced for a useful understanding of the concepts they represent. These terms are listed at the end of each chapter and are defined in the text.

Review Questions

Each of the short chapters closes with a series of five thought-provoking questions that urge the reader to rethink the concepts just studied. Some also tap students' creativity and problem-solving abilities as they encourage students to think beyond the confines of the chapters. *Multiple Choice* questions provide another method of quick review of the main points of the chapter.

Case Studies

At the end of each chapter is a case study that is based on situations and job sites with which students can identify. Rather than focusing only on huge corporations that might seem abstract and distant, these cases are drawn from situations in all types of jobs in various workplace settings. Questions at the end of the case ask students to apply concepts learned in the text to the case situation.

Instructor's Resource Manual

This teaching aid includes teaching suggestions for each chapter, sample methods of course presentation for different situations, answers and guidelines for all text Review Questions and to all Case Questions. Additional multiple choice and true/false questions on each chapter are also included.

Acknowledgements

We would like to thank some of the many people who helped us in the writing and production of this book. We especially appreciate the contributions of Carla Tishler and Bess Deck, our managing editors at Mirror Press, and Maggie Rathke, the Project Supervisor at Irwin Publishing, for their many hours of work on the manuscript. We wish Carla great success in her new position. We thank David Helmstadter, president of Mirror Press, for his faith and continuing patience with us, and we wish to thank the following reviewers for their contributions to the text: Marvin L. Copes, Kentucky Tech, Kentucky; Ron Kinsman, Great Lakes Junior College, Michigan; and Mary D. Tranquillo, St. Petersburg Junior College, Clearwater, Florida. Finally, we wish to thank our spouses, Robert Evans and Ruth Lamberton for their support and help during the writing of this book.

Contents

YOUR SKILLS AND THE GROUP

PART TWO

Chapter 12

Improving Climate: The Indoor Weather of the Workplace   103

Chapter 13

Hey! Are You Listening?   111

Chapter 14

About Those Nonverbals!   121

Chapter 15

Learning to Communicate in Other Cultures   131

Chapter 16

Watch for Hidden Agendas   141

YOUR SKILLS AND SPECIAL ISSUES IN HUMAN RELATIONS

PART
Three

PERSONAL SKILL BUILDING

PART

One

1

1

Chapter

How Is Your Self-Esteem Today?

Sandy has been working at a small insurance company for nearly four years. From the beginning, she has felt inadequate and always has been looking for her manager's approval. Before she landed this job, she used to tell herself, "I'll like myself a lot better when I finally get a good job." For some reason, though, she still has trouble liking herself three years later. "Now, if I can just make supervisor, I know, I'll feel better about myself," she reflects. Today is the big day; she has been appointed supervisor of the claims department. "Now, at last I'm somebody," Sandy thinks to herself. "Finally, I'm not going to have to feel inferior to everyone else!" Before the day is over, though, Sandy finds those inadequacy feelings are stronger than ever. "What am I going to do?" she asks her best friend that evening. "Nothing I do seems to help me like myself, including promotions, raises, new boyfriends—nothing."

Sandy's case is, sadly, not unusual. If you're like most people, you could like yourself a lot better than you do. Liking and having confidence in yourself is called **self-esteem.** For several often confusing reasons, most of us don't like ourselves as well as we should. Once you can see that problem in yourself, it's also rewarding to notice that most of the people around you act the way they do because they don't like themselves very well either. A careful look at the issue of self-esteem can help us better understand both ourselves and others.

Have you ever noticed that it is often hard to like people who don't like themselves? If you are going to work successfully with other people in any job setting, you must begin by liking and accepting yourself. Only when we like and accept ourselves can we relax and accept those around us. And only then can they like and accept us enough to achieve the goals that we both want to achieve. The workplace can thrive when it is made up of people who feel comfortable with themselves.

If you're going to be a success at whatever you try, you must *like yourself* enough to believe you can succeed. Of course, the achievement itself will help your self-esteem once it happens. But, since you need the self-esteem to achieve the goal in the first place, that's not much help right now, is it? It's as if you need the result to make the result happen. What a trap to be caught in!

Why do some people have low self-esteem? The answer is complicated, and it involves a lot of negatives that most of us received as children. With only the best of intentions, our parents were always there to remind us on a regular basis just how imperfect we were. Also, our playmates and other peers weren't always supportive. **Peer pressure** was strong, and it often took a great deal of work to "measure up." Many of us never did—or at least never felt that we measured up. For example, perhaps you weren't good at some sport or activity as a child. Certain members of your peer group probably judged you as "unworthy" because of that.

Another factor involves the **norms of society**. Most of Western culture is based on conformity, that is, living up to other people's expectations. Society punishes us for being different. Those who do not fulfill the **conformist expectations** of society—and it's easy not to—often allow themselves to feel that they are "wrong," "inferior," or even "bad."

DEVELOPING A MORE POSITIVE OPINION OF YOURSELF

Let's look at some ways to escape this self-esteem trap and learn to develop a more positive opinion of ourselves:

1. **Accept yourself as you are.**   The beginning point is *to accept yourself just as you are now.* This is often known as **self-acceptance.** Many people put off liking themselves by telling themselves things

such as, "When I'm rich, I'll like myself better." (Or "when I get promoted," or "when I marry a really attractive person," or "when I graduate from college.") These statements reflect a desire to postpone life—at least life as you would really like it to be. Take this first step by saying to yourself, "Although I want and expect to grow a lot in the future, I am an acceptable and worthy human being just as I am now; the changes in the future will simply make me even better—and happier."

2. Find out where you want to be.   Having **realistic, attainable goals** can help self-esteem immensely. You must set some goals that are possible, but have never put the time or effort into achieving. Be sure that these goals reflect your real interests—the real you. Set time lines for achievement of your goals. Include both short- and long-term goals. Ask yourself, "What do I want in the next year?" "What do I want in the next five years?" and "What do I want to be able to reflect on with satisfaction at the end of my life?" Such goals don't need to have monetary labels; they can and should be relevant to all areas of your life.

3. Use words to change your world.   Don't underestimate the **power of language.** Words can have a strong effect on our actions and feelings. If we send other people good or bad messages about themselves, they will often respond by fulfilling the messages we send. We have all heard stories about teachers who motivated students by telling them that they could succeed, with success as the result. You also probably know of cases where the opposite happens. A teacher, parent, or other leader tells a student that he or she is a failure, and the student fails. A wise person once said, "Beware of the opinions you have of yourself, for others will surely accept them."

Our own words also can influence us in our attitudes and feelings toward ourselves. When you are facing a challenge at work, tell yourself, "I can do this and do it well." This is called **"positive self-talk."** No, it's not a magical cure, but if used consistently and seriously, it can affect both your opinion of yourself and your performance on the job. Words have power—power to change minds, to shape behavior, and to raise self-esteem.

4. Improve yourself by example.   You probably know quite a few people who seem to have better self-esteem than you have. While making sure that you don't simply imitate others, try to discover the qualities of these people—the secrets of their success. One method of **learning by example** is to read biographies of people who have accomplished great deeds against heavy odds. You will likely discover that they overcame obstacles to the growth of their self-esteem. Examples from others' lives also can help you feel less lonely in your pursuit of stronger self-esteem.

5. Do a personal inventory. Write a list of the abilities that you now have. Include in this **personal inventory** the abilities that you should cultivate more and would like to work on, but which low self-esteem has prevented you from developing. If you draw a blank, ask someone who knows you well to help you create the list. Once the list is finished, think of it as a new part of your self-esteem building kit.

From this list, choose the skill that you would most enjoy developing, and start developing it right away—today, if you can. This could be a musical talent, a leadership ability, a writing ability; there are many possibilities. Once you have chosen the part of you that you want to develop, don't let a day go by without pursuing it in some way.

6. Stop putting things off. Procrastination, or intentionally putting off doing something that needs to be done, is a major enemy of good self- esteem. When projects remain uncompleted or work is put off, your feelings about yourself are likely to become self-punishing. When you are punishing yourself, no one else has to—your self-esteem is eroded already. Also, self-punishing people usually don't perform well on the job.

7. Remember the needs of other people. Part of liking ourselves is having the ability to accept and like those around us. While working on your own self-esteem, be sure that you don't forget the often intense esteem needs of other people in your life. Whatever your walk of life or organizational relationship to others in your workplace, you influence them more than you think. Watch that influence; monitor it regularly. Most important—don't devalue other people.

OVERCOMING REJECTION

One major challenge to our self-esteem is rejection. We all have been rejected by someone important to us. That rejection usually leads to our "trying harder" to get the rejecting person to accept us.

This process, however, often sets us up for a second rejection. When we are rejected again, as we usually are, our self-esteem receives a double blow.

For many of us, fear of rejection is one of our greatest fears. Whenever we fear something, we tend to have many methods ready for **overcoming rejection.** Some people react to rejection by rejecting others in various ways. Others seek to avoid the situation altogether. Still others choose to fight back—to get even. All of these behaviors have negative side effects. Worst of all, they don't improve our self-esteem.

OVERCOMING CRITICISM

We are often sensitive to criticism because we receive it as a form of rejection. Once we have placed these factors in focus, we have taken a big step in **overcoming criticism.** We should be able to see that criticism never should affect our self-esteem. If it does, it happens because we are seeking approval from others as a source of positive self-esteem. True self-esteem is strong, independent, and self-reliant.

When someone criticizes you, make sure that the criticism is meant to be destructive. Many people criticize for positive reasons and from positive motives without being aware that their behavior is threatening. They need help in self-awareness (another chapter in this book). The next step is to ask yourself, "Is there any reason I should allow this criticism to lower my opinion of myself?" The answer is almost certainly going to be no.

SELF-ESTEEM AND GROWTH

Please don't get the idea that we are offering magic formulas that will instantly raise your self-esteem level permanently. Your feelings of self-worth can grow steadily as you use the techniques mentioned here. For most of us, however, the growth process never really ends. Many middle-aged and elderly people report that although they feel better about themselves now than they did in the past, they still have a long way to go before they can say that they feel completely and consistently satisfied with their own worth. Getting out of focus at times is part of being human.

Don't set a deadline for gaining perfect self-esteem. It probably won't happen, simply because we are never perfect—just human. Our comfort with ourselves will increase with time only as we consciously work on it. Simply growing older doesn't do the job, either. For many people, growth in self-esteem is a life-long process.

Key Terms

self-esteem

peer pressure

norms of society

conformist
  expectations

self-acceptance

realistic, attainable
  goals

power of language

positive self-talk

learning by
  example

personal inventory

procrastination

overcoming
  rejection

overcoming
  criticism

Review Questions

1. Why do so many of us suffer from low self-esteem even when we have visible, undeniable proof that we are worthwhile?
2. Which of the hints in this chapter for avoiding the self-esteem trap do you think might work best in your life? Why?
3. Explain the function and importance of positive self-talk. How can this practice help build your self-esteem?
4. How is a healthy level of self-esteem important to success in life?
5. How does the tendency toward conformity in our society hurt us when we are trying to increase our self-esteem?

Multiple Choice

1. Healthy self-esteem is essential for:
   a. Personal growth
   b. Career success
   c. Happiness
   d. All of the above
2. What is wrong with Sandy, the claims supervisor in the opening vignette?
   a. She has abnormally low self-esteem.

    b. She has abnormally high self-esteem.

    c. She is typical of many people trying to succeed in life.

    d. She doesn't realize how high her self-esteem really is.

3. The *first* step toward building healthy self-esteem is:

    a. Accept yourself as you now are.

    b. Imitate other people.

    c. Stop putting things off.

    d. Stop criticizing others.

4. "I can do this, and do it well" is an example of:

    a. A position statement

    b. A position affirmation

    c. Positive self-talk

    d. A statement of low self-esteem

5. For many of us, one of our worst fears is:

    a. Fear of being seen crying.

    b. Fear of large crowds or mobs.

    c. Fear of being liked by the wrong people.

    d. Fear of rejection.

Case 1–1

Stage Fright

Raul Flores was a young executive in a midsized manufacturing plant. Although he often felt overshadowed by his peers, Raul seemed to get along pretty well unless he was asked to give an oral presentation of some kind. In the past two weeks, he had been chosen to give two 15-minute presentations.

As the day of torment approached, Raul began finding it hard to sleep. When he finally did drop off, he would often wake up, sometimes with his head pounding. Then he would imagine himself becoming tongue-tied during the presentation, and being forced to sit down because he couldn't go on. The aftermath he pictured was even worse. He imagined that the people he worked with would laugh behind his back and cease to have any respect for him. In another of his frequent wide-awake nightmares, he managed to get through the talk, but everyone thought it was simple-minded and boring. He could hear the voices of his colleagues when he walked past the coffee room. He had become the butt of their favorite jokes.

Finally, the day before the first presentation, Raul decided to see the company counselor. Although he felt ridiculous admitting what was happening to him, Raul realized that he needed to do something or the worst would really happen. The counselor was extremely understanding. Raul found that talking the problem out with her helped calm him down a bit. He was relieved when she told him that dozens of people in the company had come to her with the same problem.

1. Pretend for a moment that you are the counselor. What else will you say to Raul? What will you not say to him? Why?

2. To what extent was Raul's problem probably related to low self-esteem?

3. If you have "stage fright," what steps do you take to get over the problem?

2

Showing Others Who You Really Are

"He's a real phony," one worker says about another. "You never know what he's really thinking." He'll smile and tell you everything is fine just before he stabs you in the back." Have you heard this before? Many of us complain about other people when we feel that they aren't acting "real" or genuine. Yet, the workplace is often structured in a way that discourages everyone—managers and employees alike—from being who we really are.

After all, it's safer to smile and agree than it is to say what we really believe or feel. Often we are nearly as reluctant to reveal the truth about ourselves to our equals in the organization as to the managers who have power over us. Why? What are we afraid of? There are many reasons, most of which are related to fear.

If fear is the central reason for our reluctance to be ourselves, shouldn't we ask just what we are afraid of? Maybe we're not willing to admit that fear is a factor in our case (and sometimes it's not). It's a good question, just the same. A question such as this requires quite a lot of honesty and self-evaluation. Fear has more influence on our behavior than most of us are willing to admit, as we will see in the next chapter.

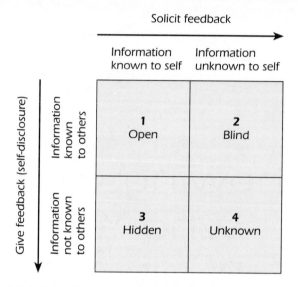

Figure 2–1   Johari Window

SOURCE: Joseph Luft. Groups Process: Introduction to Groups Dynamics (Palo Alto, CA: National Press, 1970).

SELF-DISCLOSURE

For human relations in the workplace to be effective, a high level of self-disclosure is necessary. You are likely thinking, "But wait a minute; there are some parts of myself that I'm not about to share with anyone." Of course there are. That's normal. If you started to tell all the facts of your personal life to everyone at work, you would do more harm than good to the cause of effective human relations. That would be called "overdisclosing." It overwhelms and usually embarrasses others.

Figure 2–1 is a diagram known as the Johari Window. It compares the four areas of self-knowledge based on how much we know about ourselves with how much we show others. The open pane is what we are focusing on here. As you become better acquainted with others, this pane should become larger and larger, making the others smaller. It won't ever cover the whole diagram, though, because we all need some of the hidden pane if only for privacy's sake, and we all will continue to have "blind" spots—the blind pane on the Johari Window, or areas that others can see but that we can't—though they should become fewer and fewer. The unknown pane contains areas that we don't see in ourselves and that others haven't noticed.

As you can see, it's important to know when to stop—how far to go without disclosing more of yourself than you should. Self-disclosure is a bit like walking a tightrope. On one side of the rope is too much disclosure; on the other side is too little. "Being real" involves making frequent decisions that keep us from falling from the tightrope. A few basic principles will help in making those decisions.

1. **Consider the expectations of others.**   We can usually tell how much of our true selves others want us to disclose by noticing how much they disclose of themselves to others, especially to us. Although you will find exceptions, most of us send messages on the intensity level that we expect, even hope, to get back.

Expectation levels vary from individual to individual and from place to place. For example, Jeanne moves from a company with a very closed culture, one that discouraged self-disclosure and encouraged game-playing. When she enters her new workplace, she soon finds that her co-workers of both sexes tend to share more of their personal lives with each other than she is used to. After a few weeks, Jeanne is a part of the new organization and has learned to be comfortable with it.

Not only will you find such variations between organizations, you will also find that different geographical locations will foster self-disclosure more than others. In the United States, people in the Midwest tend to have expectations of higher self-disclosure than those in New England. Some localities, even neighborhoods within such regions, will often provide exceptions to the regional rule. Take note of the self-disclosure patterns of your region.

2. **Pay attention to timing.**   *When* you self-disclose is just as important as where and to whom. This is called timing disclosure. For example, Josh has just been hired at Amalgamated Industries. During lunchtime on the first day, he shares with five of his co-workers that he is a recently divorced single parent. Ignoring raised eyebrows, Josh launches into a detailed narrative of a painful divorce. Someone changes the subject at his first long pause. He fi-

nally gets the hint that he is **overdisclosing** and drops the subject. He later finds out that such self-disclosure is just as acceptable here as it had been in other environments where he had worked; Josh just didn't give his co-workers enough time in terms of their own expectations. They needed to get to know him better in other areas of his life before hearing such personal details.

3. Have a reason for any unusual self-disclosing. Before you communicate with anyone, an important question to ask yourself is, "What is the purpose of this communication?" You will certainly think twice about what you say if you determine your own true intentions. Are you trying to make yourself look better? Are you trying to find a common ground with others? Are you trying to stimulate some self-disclosure from the listener by setting the pace? Without much trouble you can probably find several other relevant questions to ask in analyzing any conversation you start.

4. Be aware of the level of the conversation. If someone else has started the conversation, it will be helpful to analyze it in terms of the Johari Window in Figure 2–1.[1] These different levels are really different levels of involvement, or commitment, to communicating. When someone in your workplace sends you a message on one level, he or she is probably expecting a reply on the same level. Your effectiveness as a communicator depends a great deal on your ability to adjust to, or change, the level of conversation. Sometimes, the level needs to be higher or lower. You can "test the water" by offering a statement or question on your desired level, then watching the reaction from the other speaker.

For example, a co-worker greets you in the morning with, "Lousy day, huh?" This is cliché conversation. However, you are concerned why this person finds a bright, sunny morning to be "lousy." You ask, "Is something wrong?" Now, the co-worker can be the one who decides whether or not to go to a different level of disclosure. The following are five levels of self-disclosure.

Level 5: Cliché conversation. This is the level that includes such expressions as "Hi, how are you?" "Nice day, isn't it?" "Hey, how about those Celtics." This is nonconversation. All speakers are safe from emotional damage; no one takes risks.

---

[1] John Powell, *Why Am I Afraid to Tell You Who I Am?* (Chicago: Argus Communications, 1969), pp. 50–62.

Level 4: Reporting facts about others. Though this level goes beyond the clichés, no real self-disclosure is taking place. The topics cover "what so-and-so is doing," but they don't include personal evaluations; so we remain relatively safe from attack and reveal little of our own opinions or feelings.

Level 3: Expressing ideas and judgments. This level requires some honesty and puts us at risk with the other speaker or speakers. However, the risks aren't really demanding ones, and the deeper parts of our personality are still not available to others.

Level 2: The "gut level." This level allows the other person to know what is in your "gut" as well as your head. We not only share our ideas and thoughts with the other person, but allow them to understand how we honestly feel about the subject. This is true self-disclosure.

Level 1: Peak communication. This is that wonderful conversational level that we achieve only with certain people and then only once in a while. In this exciting context, we seem to enter the world of the other person, feeling similar feelings and enjoying mutual understanding. Because this level is achieved only occasionally, we should think of level 2 as the highest level usually achieved.

If the conversation is on the cliché level and seems to remain there, you would be wise to recognize its position and move in a careful, timely fashion to the level you find appropriate to the time, the place, and the people involved. Level 2, the "gut" level, is the best position in which to spend most of our time. By using this level as often as possible, we can improve our relationships with others and enjoy greater honesty from them in return. Of course, much of routine business conversation takes place on levels 3 and 4. If that is all that's needed, be aware of and be satisfied with it.

5. **Try to see yourself as others see you.**   Before self-disclosing ask, "What does this person see when looking at me?" This might sound a bit self-conscious. Well, it is. It is also an important first step towards *empathy* with other people. Empathy is the ability to "put yourself in the other's place" to understand feelings and ideas better. This step can guard against the defensiveness that we often find both in others and in ourselves: If I can see what there is in my conversation or my behavior that made you act defensively, then I am more likely to avoid the mistake of reacting with my own defensiveness.

For example, Nancy, a new employee who has a lower position in the workplace than you have, sees you as a big, threatening person who might be out to hurt her in some way. Once you understand how you are perceived by Nancy, you can modify your self-disclosure to keep from accidentally threatening her security as one way to combat her defensiveness. If we can see ourselves through the eyes of others, all of our communications are likely to improve.

Your second step toward improved human relations, then, is disclosing who you really are. You will find that most others will accept you better, relationships will improve, and communications will be clearer and easier on both the sending and the receiving ends. When people know what they are dealing with, suspicions tend to dissolve and constructive work can be done.

Key Terms

self-disclosure

Johari Window

open pane

hidden pane

blind pane

unknown pane

expectation levels

timing disclosure

overdisclosing

five levels of self-disclosure:
5. cliché conversation
4. reporting facts about others
3. ideas and judgments
2. "gut level"
1. peak communication

Review Questions

1. Explain how the Johari Window can help you understand your own level of self-disclosure.
2. Why is *timing* an important element in self-disclosure? Provide an example of bad timing from your own experience.
3. List the five steps toward better self-disclosure. Can you think of an example of each from your own life?
4. What is overdisclosing? What kind of damage can it do? Discuss.
5. Why is the "gut level" the best level of self-disclosure on which to be most of the time?

Multiple Choice

1. For human relations in the workplace to be effective:
   a. The manager must always solve organizational problems.
   b. A high level of self-disclosure is necessary.

   c. All workers must keep important information among themselves only.

   d. Everyone needs to know all of everyone else's business.

2. Which of the following is *not* one of the four "panes" of the Johari Window?

   a. Hidden pane

   b. Blind pane

   c. Unconscious pane

   d. Open pane

3. The most important benefit of communicating on the gut level is that:

   a. Everyone always answers you on the same level.

   b. Relationships are likely to grow stronger.

   c. Everyone can understand you, even those who speak no English.

   d. You as the speaker are always completely in charge of the situation.

4. After a relationship has been developed, which of the following happens?

   a. All four of the Johari Window panes enlarge.

   b. The open pane of the Johari Window becomes larger.

   c. The hidden pane becomes larger.

   d. The benevolent pane enlarges.

5. When Arturo Alvarez took a bus across town, a young man sat down next to him. In 20 minutes he had told Arturo a short version of his life story. Arturo felt uncomfortable. What was the stranger's mistake?

   a. He included too much detail.

   b. He summarized the story too rapidly.

   c. He talked too fast.

   d. He overdisclosed.

Case 2–1

Trouble in the Shop

Jack LaChance, a mechanic in a transmission shop, returns to work after a sick day and finds that several of his tools are missing. When he asks around, he finds that his friend Tony Palmeri, who usually works on the other end of the shop, has borrowed them. "Why in the world did you take my tools without asking?" Jack yells when he sees Tony coming toward him.

Tony: Hey, we've known each other forever. I can't believe you care. I mean, here they are—well, except for the torque wrench. It doesn't seem to be reading right.

Jack: So now you've even ruined one of my tools! Man, what kind of guy are you, anyway?

Tony: I don't get it. Hey, we can fix the calibration on the torque. I've done it before; it's no big deal.

Jack: No, the big deal is that you're a thief. If you ever touch my tools again I'll give you something to remember me by.

Tony was really taken aback. During lunch, he approached Jack again. This time, he apologized. "Man, I had no idea you'd be like this, but I guess I need to say I'm sorry. Look, I'll fix the torque wrench myself after work tonight. I guess I just didn't know you felt that way about your tools. I mean, you've bought me lunch a hundred times; I thought you were one of those really generous guys."

Jack: I *am* generous—too generous. I'm always helping guys like you out because I feel sorry for you. But you walk all over me and take advantage of me the minute my back is turned. I've had it!

Tony: Excuse me, but lots of times you insisted on buying lunch and drinks, even when I offered to pay for yours.

Jack: OK, OK, let's drop it. Just keep your hands off my tools from now on.

Tony: Look, Jack, I just wish you'd have let me know about some of these feelings before, like how you feel about your tools. If you had, I guarantee I wouldn't have used them, ever.

1. How self-aware is Jack LaChance? How self-aware is Tony? What do you base your assessments on?

2. How could self-disclosure have prevented this confrontation? How could it help now? Or has it helped somewhat already?

3. What else would you do if you were Tony? Why?

Getting Rid of Fear

"I'm going to stick to the same technique I've been using," an advertising layout director says to herself. "I'm not about to try something that management is going to find fault with."

"I don't want to see this client today," a salesperson says. "It's not a good time of day, and he'll probably be more likely to buy tomorrow."

"You know, I have some really good ideas for this new product line," a supervisor tells his colleague in another department. "But I'm not about to tell anybody about them. Every time I've offered ideas about anything around here, I've been criticized. I've learned to keep my mouth shut."

Do these three situations have anything in common? Yes, all three speakers are expressing fear—each in a different way. But here's the strange part: It's unlikely that any of the three realizes that they are feeling fear. In our workaday lives, we react to many situations with fear as our chief motivation and *we don't even know it.* For one thing, most of us don't want to admit that we are fearful, even to ourselves. Thus, our reluctance to take certain actions—or lack of action—is based on an emotion that we give another, more comfortable name, such as "being safe," "being careful," or "playing good politics." The truth is that our workplaces are full of fear. The question is how to get rid of this enemy of good human relations.

COMMON FEARS

The fears that are potentially the most damaging to our human relations are those that have to do with self-doubt and with other people and their reactions to us. Most of these common fears come from low self-esteem. We have a fear of others because we lack confidence; we lack confidence because we don't like ourselves as well as we should.

These self-fears and social fears are largely exaggerated. Most of them have little or no basis in reality. Certainly, we might be rejected by others, or we might say the wrong thing in a social situation. The exaggeration of the fear is not that the outcome is unlikely, simply that its results aren't as threatening as we make them out to be. The feared result might happen; but if it does, will we be destroyed? No.

We often make social fears worse by dwelling on past mistakes. One of our students tells of a night of being unable to get to sleep because of a social blunder she had made that day—one that had made her feel "totally humiliated," as she put it. After mentally punishing herself for half an hour, she began recalling other social blunders she had made during her lifetime. One by one, they revealed themselves, humiliation after humiliation, until by about 2:00 AM, she recalls, she was "ready to die."

Then she began asking herself, "How many of the people who witnessed my humiliation even remember the incident?" Going back to the events of the past, she began asking herself, "How many of those people even remember who I am?" After admitting to herself that they had probably forgotten, she turned her attention back to the most recent "humiliation" that started all this self-punishment. "They probably don't care either, and won't even remember it tomorrow," she admitted to herself. By 2:30 AM she was fast asleep, ready to awaken short of sleep, but longer on self-confidence and—most importantly—not paralyzed by fear.

CHOOSING OTHER EMOTIONS

We need to establish an important truth early in this book; that is, we as humans *choose* the emotions we are going to feel and express in a given situation. If you get angry and yell at your best friend, you have chosen anger as the emotion you will feel and express. Fear is also an emotion. When we feel fear, somewhere—though often on an unconscious level—we are choosing that emotion over other possibilities. A more constructive approach is **choosing other emotions.** Replace the emotion of fear with another, such as confidence or optimism. First, try to identify fear among your common emotions. Be honest; no one else has to know. Then ask yourself, "What can I do to control that emotion and replace it with another?"

DON'T EXPECT FEAR TO DISAPPEAR FROM YOUR LIFE

In her book, *Feel the Fear and Do it Anyway,* psychologist Susan Jeffers points out that the **persistence of fear** is a part of life, a part of growth. Though some fears can and should be "gotten rid of," the more important skill is that of learning to deal with fears realistically.[1] Many people tell themselves, "Well, I'll just give it a few days (or weeks or months) and the fear will die down. Then I'll take action." Wrong! Fears that haven't been attended to are very unlikely to go away on their own.

Henry decided to put off taking public speaking until his junior year in college. When the junior year came, he found that his problems with fear and nervousness were the same as they were his freshman year. However, when the semester of speech class was over, Henry's fears had diminished a great deal. If Henry had acted first, then expected the fear level to improve, he would have been using the strategy that usually succeeds: "Feel the fear and do it anyway."[2] You will have greater success against your fears by simply taking hold of the problem, jumping in with gritted teeth, and looking your fears in the face.

Principle 1, You will always have fear as long as you are growing. You could possibly reduce fear from your life by creating a secure environment where nothing interferes with your peace. Some have

---

[1] Susan Jeffers, *Feel the Fear and Do It Anyway* (New York: Fawcett Columbine, 1987), pp. 22–28.

[2] Jeffers, pp. 22–30.

tried, with mixed success. However, as long as you are a growing, developing human being, fear will continue to be a reality. Don't wait for the fear to go away before you act. It won't!

Principle 2, The only way to get rid of fear is to go out and do what you fear. This is **overcoming fear by action.** Remember that the "doing it" or action step has to come first. A musician friend of ours tells about the first time he performed in public. He was part of a three-set concert, and he was in the middle. Unlike the other sets, which were groups, his was a solo act—just him and his guitar. He was so petrified that he thought he would either be sick on the stage or not be able to hit a single note—maybe both. When his name was called, he took a deep breath and began. Although the first number wasn't performed to his satisfaction, the audience applauded enthusiastically. By the time his set was finished, he was actually enjoying himself—although he was still very nervous. After about four more appearances, he started looking forward to public performances. Now, years later, he says he would rather perform in front of a live audience than anything else in the world.

What if our friend had decided he would wait until the fear went away, and then try a live concert? We asked him that question. His answer: He would probably never have gotten over the fear enough to try and would to this day be another unsung musician.

Principle 3, Don't feel alone; nearly everyone experiences fears of some kind. People from all walks of life and every place on earth who must deal with it demonstrate the **universality of fear.** The professor who seems relaxed while lecturing, the musician who loves performing, the job applicant who gives the impression of confidence—all have had to grapple with fear. A voice teacher once said, "Don't let it worry you that you are nervous; being nervous means that you're intelligent enough to care about your performance." His students report being helped by that admonition just because it assured them that they were not alone.

Principle 4, Confronting fear is much less frightening than the feeling of helplessness that comes from inaction. Have you ever known someone who lived life in such a way that risks were all but eliminated? Bill was like that. He made sure he had a secure, salaried job; he never married in order to avoid the possibility of divorce. Although he often thought of two hobbies he liked reading about—motorcycling and skin diving—he avoided them both because they were "too dangerous."

In the space of a month, he had lost his secure job, and his widowed mother had a stroke. At the age of 38, he found himself job hunting and caring for an invalid mother. No longer could he be helpless. His mother was depending on him, and he had no intention of starving. Soon, Bill had a new job, one with better pay and more opportunity for advancement than his previous job. And caring for his mother proved to be a rewarding experience for him. He was shaken out of his comfort zone, and looked and felt happier as a result. He even tried both of his once-feared hobbies. Few emotions are more frightening than the feeling of helplessness. Acting in spite of our fears is the best way of **overcoming helplessness.**

DON'T TURN FEAR INTO BLAMING

When we fear something, we often trap ourselves into **blaming others.** Instead of admitting that we are afraid, we identify others in our lives who have caused us not to act or to run away from what we fear. Keith would really like to return to school to improve his career possibilities. His wife Jill, though a bit afraid of his taking such a step, is mostly supportive. He hides his own fear by telling friends, "Oh, I'd love to go back to college, but Jill is giving me too much trouble about it." If you are not doing something you believe you could or should do, check whether you're blaming someone else for your inaction. If you are, examine that blame closely. Is it realistic? Is the other person perhaps less to blame than you are letting on—both to others and to yourself?

THE "WORST POSSIBLE SCENARIO" APPROACH

Dale Carnegie, the world-famous author of *How to Win Friends and Influence People,* suggests a three-step method of reducing fear.[3]

---

[3] Dale Carnegie, *How to Stop Worrying and Start Living* (New York: Pocket Books, 1953).

Step 1—Start with the "worst possible scenario." To use this method, begin by picturing the worst outcome that could possibly result from the situation making you fearful. In nearly every case, you'll find that the worst possible scenario would be something that you could live with. You'd still be alive, you'd still be a functioning member of society, and so forth. Next, remind yourself that the worst possible outcome is not usually the most likely one to happen. Something less terrible is much more likely to take place.

Step 2—Prepare yourself for this worst possible outcome. You need to know that you are strong enough to survive this really negative possibility. Put yourself into the frame of mind that says, "I'm ready for whatever happens—even the worst that could take place."

Step 3—Proceed with a plan. Using the worst possible outcome as a kind of safety valve, put together a realistic plan that you can see yourself realistically putting into action. Plan to see the problem through to the final solution. Plan not to allow temporary setbacks to discourage you. Keep the plan in your mind, thinking about it as often as possible.

Fear will never be eliminated from your life. It shouldn't be. Expect it, anticipate it, but don't be paralyzed by it. Don't wait until the fear is gone to act. Act now. Feel the fear, but act anyway. Your acting will reduce the fear and increase your self-confidence, and thus your human relations abilities.

Key Terms

self-doubt

common fears

low-self esteem

fear of others

social fears

choosing other
  emotions

persistence of fear

overcoming fear
  by action

universality of fear

overcoming
  helplessness

blaming others

worst possible
  scenario

Review Questions

1. What are some common fears that plague many, if not most, of us?
2. "Fears that haven't been attended to are very unlikely to go away on their own." Why?
3. List the four principles of fear and show how each can "work" in your own life at work and elsewhere.
4. Explain the "worst possible scenario" approach to defeating fear. Do you see this approach working for you? Why or why not?
5. Explain the relationship between low self-esteem and fear.

Multiple Choice

1. Which of the following statements about fear is true?
   a. By taking the steps outlined in this chapter, you can get fear to disappear from your life.
   b. Many of the fears we feel every day are not even recognized as fears.
   c. We often make social fear worse by dwelling on our past social failings.
   d. The only way to get rid of fear is to go out and do whatever we are afraid of doing.
2. The fears that are the most potentially damaging to our human relations are:
   a. Those that threaten our job security.
   b. Those that threaten our family stability.
   c. Those that have to do with self-doubt and the fear of other people and their reactions to us.
   d. Those that have to do with physical danger, such as fear of heights and fear of confined spaces.
3. You will always have fear as long as you:
   a. Want success.
   b. Like yourself.
   c. Are growing.
   d. Like working.
4. If you get angry and yell at or hit someone, the fault for the incident lies with:

    a. Your kindergarten teacher who didn't teach you to control anger.

    b. Yourself, because you made the choice to react in that manner.

    c. The other person, for doing something that made you angry.

    d. Your parents, for not teaching you to deal with anger.

5. Which of the following is *not* one of the three steps of Carnegie's "worst possible scenario" approach?

    a. Start with the worst possible scenario.

    b. Prepare yourself for the best possible outcome.

    c. Prepare yourself for the worst possible outcome.

    d. Proceed with a plan.

Case 1–3

Frozen with Fear

Karen Higdom had only been in the human resources department of Arcom for two months when she was appointed to represent her department on the corporate planning team. Although she was honored at the appointment, she was frightened that she might be put on the spot and asked to respond to questions that she didn't feel qualified to answer. After the first three rather uneventful meetings had passed, the team leader asked Karen to give a presentation on future staffing policies and their long-term effect on the company.

Now Karen's fear became intense. Although the human resource manager, Jeanne Collard, offered to help her with the statistics and even with the wording of the report, Karen was frozen with fear. Not only was she having trouble sleeping at night, but she found herself wanting to resign her position, leave the company—anything to avoid that fateful presentation.

On the day before her feared speech, she asked for a private appointment with Jeanne. "Ms. Collard," Karen stammered. "I'd rather die than give this presentation." After several minutes of questions and revelations, Jeanne established that Karen was a veteran public speaker; she had even been on the debate team in her community college.

Jeanne: What's different this time?

Karen: I just don't feel like I know enough to carry this off.

Jeanne: Well, what's the worst possible thing that could happen tomorrow?

Karen: I guess they could ask me questions at the end of the presentation that I would have to say "duh" about. Even one question like that and I'd be totally humiliated.

Jeanne: Well, here's a plan. I'll be there at the end of your speech. Any questions you feel you can't answer intelligently, just refer them to me.

Karen: Great! You're a life-saver.

The next day, after a very smooth presentation, Karen handled all 12 of the questions that were asked without once using Jeanne's knowledge as a resource. "Your being there was enough," Karen told Jeanne later. "If you hadn't been there, I couldn't have pulled it off."

1. What was the basis of Karen's fears?

2. How did Jeanne use the "worst possible scenario" approach to help Karen's fears? Was that part of her approach effective? Why or why not?

3. Do you agree that if Jeanne hadn't been there, Karen might have failed? Why or why not?

Now, About that Attitude!

"Can't he tone down that **negative talk**?" one worker complains to another. "Doesn't he know that his attitude is poisoning this whole company?" "Yeah," replies the other worker, "When Joe's been around you can always tell; everybody's nastier."

Attitudes can make us or break us in the workplace and anywhere else where we are surrounded by people. Our attitudes are based on our way of looking at the world, especially the world of others. You've probably known people who always seem to find the bad side in anything that happens. Their view of the world causes them to have **negative attitudes**. Life is full of both negatives and positives. Your attitude is a choice of which of the two you decide to emphasize.

WHAT IS AN ATTITUDE?

An attitude is a state of mind based on the view we have of the world around us. That mental state sets us up to react in a certain way when anything new enters our reality. Some people call an attitude a **"state of readiness."** You are ready to react in a certain manner, based on what that condition of readiness is. Joe, for example, is ready to react negatively to everything that happens.

People like Joe are everywhere and are a constant challenge to those of us who understand the importance of human relations. Negative attitudes need to be done away with for several reasons:

- They spread like a disease. One negative attitude carrier can produce dozens—even hundreds—of other bad attitudes.
- They hurt morale. When a workplace suffers from low morale, workers are absent more often, are tardy more often, and have trouble keeping their minds on their jobs.
- They damage productivity. You would be amazed at the amount of work that can be done when everyone working on the task is positive about it. Sadly, the opposite is also true.
- They destroy fun in the workplace. Work should be fun. If it's not fun, it should be possible to transform it into fun. Bad attitudes kill that possibility.

ATTITUDE CARRIERS

Attitudes are contagious like the flu. Joe, in our opening example, carries his bad attitude wherever he goes. Because he is so very negative, others notice and dislike him. Some people's negativism, though, is more subtle, less easy to see. When you spend time around someone like that, you will often wonder, "Why am I feeling so negative?" The answer is that you have been influenced by someone else more than you had suspected.

When you find yourself with a negative attitude, ask yourself where the attitude came from. If you can trace its source—and often you can—work on it from the source. For example, if you are working with someone whose negative attitude has rubbed off on you, focus on the actions and words of that person, making sure that these **attitude carriers** don't turn you sour as well.

Maybe the attitude started when you got out of bed this morning. Maybe someone cut you off in traffic, crowded you in the bus, or scowled at you on the sidewalk. It's amazing how sometimes very small happenings can trigger a negative attitude. Attitudes do get out of focus. Noticing that they do is one of the first steps toward correcting the problem.

ATTITUDE ADJUSTMENTS

Once you have admitted that your attitude has gotten out of focus, start working on an **attitude adjustment**. Define where the problem came from. Was it one of the "small happenings" mentioned above? Or was it something you can't put your finger on? If you absolutely can't understand why your attitude is out of focus, go to the next step. Joke. Try to see something humorous in your surroundings, your situation, or yourself. Share your humor with someone else if that seems appropriate.

Use whatever works for you. Some people have found that meditation works. For others, some cheerful music does the trick. Still others find that simply sharing their feelings with someone they trust pulls them out of the doldrums. Find the gimmick that works for you and use it when you need it.

Whenever you're dealing with others at this point, be careful to send them positive messages. Until you get your mood into focus, don't confuse others by exposing them to the fuzziness of your own lens. Finally, test yourself to see if your attitude has really become focused. Use the attitude adjustment checklist on the next page as a test to see whether your attitude is in adjustment.

BUILDING A POSITIVE ATTITUDE

Beyond simply getting out of focus, we all need to think in terms of overall building of **positive attitudes**—toward work, toward others, and toward ourselves. The following are some tips that will help in that process.

1. Learn to take the optimist's approach.   You've probably heard the old saying about the pessimist who sees a glass of water as half empty and the optimist who sees it as half full. The two characters in the saying probably weren't born with their differing viewpoints. Becoming an optimist is a choice we make in our lives. When two possibilities present themselves, make the conscious

Attitude Adjustment Checklist

Acknowledge that your attitude is out of focus.
Define where the problem came from.
Joke. It's amazing what humor can do to change your perspective.
Use whatever methods help you to think more positive thoughts.
Send messages that deny the negative thoughts and don't drag others down.
Test your mood to see whether the change is permanent.

choice to choose the more positive one. Choose to see a half-full glass rather than a half-empty one. Sometimes the emotion that triggers our pessimism is fear (see Chapter 3).

2. **Don't let the attitude carriers get to you.**   Although you might not be able to correct negative attitudes in other people, you can still do a great deal to keep their negative attitudes from affecting you. Remind yourself that the attitude carrier is the one with the problem. Tell yourself, "I will not allow his or her problem to become my own." Remember that there is a limit to how much you can do to change someone else's attitude, but few limits to how much you can do to change your own.

3. **Don't let life push you around.**   People with positive attitudes are in control of themselves and their own lives. Don't let either situations or other people control your destiny. Self-esteem is a key to personal control. Believe that you are good enough to make important decisions that affect your life. Then make them. Following this step doesn't mean that you should push others around, nor does it mean that you should manipulate your environment to an unfair advantage. It does mean being in charge of your own life.

4. **Don't allow yourself to be controlled by your feelings.**   Feelings—the emotional parts of ourselves—can and should be controlled by our minds. When we do not have control of feelings, emotions rule. If you were being tried for a crime, would you want the judge in the case to be totally ruled by emotions, or to use his or her mind to weigh the evidence carefully? When we allow emotions to control our destinies, we often make shortsighted decisions and find ourselves in situations we could have avoided with some thoughtful planning.

5. **Become goal oriented.**   Goal orientation—having a set of realistic and attainable goals—can work wonders on your self-esteem as well as on your general attitudes. When you set personal goals, be sure to choose goals that are tough but attainable—just out of your present reach. Then, never accomplish one goal without setting a new one to take its place.

DON'T WORRY, BE HAPPY

Where do you think happiness comes from? Some recent studies have shown that people who have happy attitudes get their happiness from being in control of their own choices. As oversimplified as it may seem, *we can choose to be happy.* In a 10-year study at the National Institute on Aging, researchers found that people who had been happy 10 years before were still happy, regardless of either negative or positive events in their lives.[1]

Psychologist David Myers lists four characteristics that people with happy attitudes seem to have in common:

1. **Good self-esteem.** People who love themselves are happier than those who don't. Work on the material from Chapter 1 of this book and you'll be taking your first step toward a happy attitude.

2. **Optimism.** Being an optimist leads you to choose a happy attitude over an unhappy one. Optimism means that you are the person who says, "I can do it," "You have great potential," and "Today is going to be a good day."

3. **Extroversion.** Happy people are usually outgoing. An extrovert is someone whose behavior is directed outward, toward others, rather than always inward, toward oneself. Notice that this characteristic—extroversion—is closely related to self-esteem levels. Healthy self-esteem will keep you from being overly preoccupied with yourself and will help direct your communications toward others.

4. **Personal control.** Happy people are in control of their own lives. When someone else controls your choices in life, either large or small, your happiness level is lower. Studies with prison inmates show that even small freedoms—such as room arrangement or menu choice—will improve attitudes noticeably.

CHANGING BAD ATTITUDES

When you are confronted with other people who have negative attitudes, your best method of changing those attitudes is often by influence and example. This is especially true when you can't pinpoint the reasons for the negative attitude you've discovered. Sometimes, however, the reasons are apparent. When you know where the negatives are coming from, you can attack them at the source.

For example, Seth starts work in a new office where everyone seems to be unhappy. He soon finds out that workers are hearing

---

[1] David G. Myers, "The Secret of Happiness," *Psychology Today* 25 (July-Aug. 1992), p. 38.

rumors daily that a layoff is about to take place. Seth carefully begins asking every manager to whom he has access for more information on the layoff. He soon finds that a dozen workers are to be let go, but all are in another division of the company and that no layoffs are anticipated in his part of the company. His counterrumor helps quench the negative rumor, and soon attitudes begin to improve.

If you are a supervisor or manager, you are in an even better position than Seth to discover the sources of an attitude problem. You can also more likely influence the attitudes of those who work for you; negative attitudes often start at the top, then trickle down to the workers.

Few issues in human relations are as important as the attitude you project. Check it out; stay in touch with your own feelings. When your attitude gets out of focus, refocus as soon as possible. Be the manager, fellow worker, or friend who carries the positive attitudes. Every other area of human relations will improve for you and for those you work with.

Key Terms

negative talk   positive attitudes   happy attitudes
negative attitudes   personal control   optimism
state of readiness   control of feelings   extroversion
attitude carriers   goal-orientation
attitude adjustment

Review Questions

1. One definition of *attitude* is "a state of readiness." Explain that definition.
2. What are the reasons why negative attitudes are harmful in the workplace?
3. Explain the concept and process of "attitude adjustment."
4. What are the five steps in building a positive attitude? Explain each one, using an example.
5. Do you think a "happy attitude" is something you can really develop?

Multiple Choice

1. An attitude is a state of mind based on:
   a. Our beliefs and prejudices.
   b. The view we have of the world around us.
   c. Our concept of workplace productivity.
   d. Our beliefs about leadership.
2. Once we have admitted that our attitude gets out of focus, we should begin working on:
   a. Getting even
   b. Finding out how it happened
   c. Attitude adjustment
   d. Becoming a leader
3. Which of the following is *not* one of the steps in building a positive attitude?
   a. Learn to take the optimist's approach.
   b. Don't let life push you around.
   c. Don't allow yourself to be controlled by feelings.
   d. Discover who got you into a negative attitude to begin with.
4. Psychologist David Myers lists four characteristics that people with a happy attitude have in common. Which of the following is *not* one of them?
   a. Good self-esteem
   b. Optimism
   c. Introversion
   d. Personal control
5. Happy people are usually:
   a. Lazy
   b. Introverted
   c. Outgoing
   d. Futureless

Case 4–1

The Efficient Waitress

Linda Dean was a waitress in a downtown coffee shop. As she passed one of her tables, she saw three quarters that the last diners had left. "Whadda ya know," she said to herself, "They actually left a tip, if you can call it that. These retired people—if they don't have enough money to tip, why do they go out to eat in the first place!" On her way back to the kitchen she saw Judy, a waitress in her early twenties. "Whistling and laughing again," Linda complained to herself, "You'd think that kid didn't have any work to do. She makes so much small talk with the customers, it's no wonder she doesn't move 'em fast enough."

Back in the kitchen, Linda was still mumbling under her breath. The manager, Phil Henderson, asked her if something was wrong. Linda's reply was a facial expression that read: Don't bug me. Yesterday, Phil had called her into his office to discuss her treatment of customers.

Phil: You need to smile more often, be more willing to help each customer with whatever problem they might have.

Linda: I'm the most efficient waitress in this restaurant. I challenge you to prove I'm not.

Phil: I agree that you're extremely efficient, fast, and thorough.

Linda: [almost shouting] What your problem, then? Let me get back to work; you're wasting my time.

Phil watched Linda thoughtfully as she walked from the kitchen. "It's too bad," he said to nobody in particular, "But I'm going to have to fire my most efficient employee. Too bad she can't see that efficiency isn't the whole story."

1. How does Linda's behavior illustrate the importance of attitude to success in the workplace?

2. What specific problems are Linda's negative attitudes causing in this restaurant?

3. If you were Phil Henderson, would you try some other course of action before firing Linda? If so, what?

5

What Do Values Have to Do with Anything?

Bonnie and her daughter Hannah were having a cup of coffee. Hannah had graduated from high school a few years ago. She had always been interested in writing, but remained dissatisfied with her job options.

"Mom, I just don't know what to try next. I can't seem to find a job that I like. If I find one that makes money, I don't like the work. If I find one that I like doing, I don't make enough money to live on."

Bonnie said, "Well, Hannah, I've told you before, I could always get you hired at the nuclear power plant where I work. You could work in technical writing or even write the public relations pieces, like the press releases or the newsletter."

"Mom! I've told you before! I could never work for a nuclear power plant—that goes against all my values!"

What are values? Where do we get them? Do we hold values only as individuals, or can groups hold values, too? Why is it important to understand our own values and the values of other people? These are some of the questions we will answer in this chapter.

VALUES

Values can be defined as the importance or worth we attach to different objects or issues in our lives. These can include activities or any frame of mind that we consider important. We are not always aware at the surface of what our values are. Together, all of our values are called a **value system.** Individuals all have their own value systems, but organizations and corporations have value systems, too. The value system of an organization is called its **corporate culture.** We often clash with another person or with an organization because our values are different. To succeed in an organization or in a relationship (either at work or in our personal life), it is important to accept and understand other people's values as well as our own.

WHERE DO WE GET OUR VALUES?

Our personal values begin to form in childhood. They come from our parents, our culture and society, and the people around us while we are growing up. Our values can change during our lives, but deeply held values (such as those related to religion or political and economic views) may not change.

Other factors that affect our values are our religion, the political views and activities of our parents, our socioeconomic class, our education level, and the mass media (such as television). Even the events happening in the world at the time we grew up help form our values. For example, you may know people who grew up during the Great Depression of the 1930s. People who grew up in conditions of poverty during the Depression typically save extra food and many other things, and they don't spend much money on luxuries. The grandmother of one of the authors of this book canned or froze fruit, vegetables, and jam well into her 70s. She also knit or sewed clothing and blankets because "it saves money," even though it would have been faster, easier, and even cheaper in the long run to buy these products.

EXAMPLES OF VALUE SYSTEMS

We all hold different value systems, but there are several types of value systems that are common among different people. See if you fit into any of the types of value systems described here, based on the theories of Edward Spranger, a sociologist, written earlier this century.[1]

1. Some people value thinking, learning, and discovering truth. **Theoretical people,** or people who are philosophical, observe what is going on around them, and think events through, trying to put their ideas into a system.

2. **Economic people** value personal needs, production, and wealth, which they regard as more important than social needs or artistic values.

3. **Aesthetic people** value beauty and harmony. Artistic form and vision are important to them.

4. **Social people** value relationships with others. Kindness, unselfishness, and cooperation are important to these people.

5. **Political people** are motivated by power. Their values center on influence, fame, and power.

6. **Religious people** value unity, or spirituality. They try to understand the universe as a whole and relate to it in a meaningful way.

VALUES AND WORK

According to some social scientists, the values that people in the United States have held about work have changed over the past few decades. Most working Americans now feel that the kind of work they do is something to value. They also value their leisure time, and they value being treated in a personalized and humane way at work. These values help give us a sense of self-esteem, a sense of identity, and the feeling that our lives somehow have a positive impact on others. Because we hold these values, we also place more importance these days on individual freedom of choice, a flexible work organization, and a feeling of closeness to our community and to nature.

---

[1] Edward Spranger, *Types of Men* (New York: Harcourt Brace Jovanovich, Johnson Reprints, 1928 orig. pub. date), 1989.

ORGANIZATIONAL VALUES

Values are what give an organization a basis for its purpose and goals. **Organizational values** evolve over time as an organization develops its focus. Leaders in an organization symbolize what the company stands for, and they can influence how values are formed. Organizational values can also affect relationships in the organization. People's importance to the company will be judged on their shared values, and this will affect who is promoted. Shared values also will affect who becomes friends at work, and which people choose to work together. What does your company stand for? What does it take pride in? If you are feeling frustrated or unhappy at work, it may be because your personal values conflict with the organizational values at work. The value system of an organization becomes the organization's corporate culture.

WHAT ARE YOUR PERSONAL VALUES?

We often have a hard time knowing what our own values really are. Sometimes we want to be accepted and fit in with others, so we ignore our own values. Ask yourself, "Do my values change depending on where I am and who I'm with?" If the answer is yes, then you may not be paying enough attention to your own values. The questions that follow are part of the Rath Test, which was developed by a well-known expert on values, Louis Rath.[2] This test can help people find out whether the values they *think* they have are the ones they really do have. Take any one of the values you consider to be important in your life, and ask yourself these seven questions about that value.

1. *Did I choose this value myself, with no pressure from anyone else?*   Do you hold a value because someone else, or a group, provided you with it? For example, did you join the Republican or Democratic political party because your parents belonged to that party? If the value originated somewhere else, did it become your own value along the way?

---

[2] Louis Rath, Merrill Haron, and Sidney Simon, *Values and Teaching* (Columbus, OH: Charles Merrill Publishers, 1976).

2. *Did I choose this value from a group of alternatives?*   Did you notice that other choices were possible, or did you just accept the value without looking in another direction? For example, did you accept the idea of corporal punishment in schools, such as spanking, without considering whether other kinds of discipline might be successful and more acceptable to parents and to school district staff?

3. *Have I considered the consequences of my choice?*   Having a strong belief in a value is likely to have consequences in your life, and not all of these consequences will be positive. For example, if you decide that you do not want to have friends outside of your own religious or ethnic group, are you ready to live without some wonderful friendships and possibly even some family members?

4. *Do I like and respect this value?*   Values that you hold strongly will be motivating. They will be values you respect, and you will respect other people who hold the same values. For example, if you believe that environmental issues are important, you will be motivated to "reduce, reuse, and recycle," and you will respect people who work at a recycling center.

5. *Will I defend this value publicly?*   Will you be able to defend your value in front of people who might disagree with you or might even dislike you because of your belief? For example, if you believe strongly in equal rights for women and nonwhite ethnic minority groups, will you be able to speak up to your co-workers when they are telling racist or sexist jokes at work?

6. *Will I base my behavior on this value?*   Remember the old saying, "Do as I say and not as I do?" It is much easier to say what we believe than it is to follow through. Will you be able to make your value a part of the way you act in everyday life? For example, do you tell your children that stealing, lying and cheating are wrong, yet you keep that extra dollar the cashier gave you by mistake, "fudge" a little on your income taxes, "roll" through a stop sign, or jaywalk?

7. *Is this value consistent throughout my life?*   If you really hold this value, you should see it affecting all areas of your life, past and present. It should be long lasting. For example, if your political beliefs are strongly conservative, you should be able to look at your past voting record and see a consistent pattern of voting for the conservative side of issues.

Using the Rath Test, you should be able to separate your *true* values from those that you only *thought* were strong in your life.

Key Terms

values

value system

corporate culture

theoretical people

economic people

aesthetic people

social people

political people

religious people

organizational
   values

Review Questions

1. Is there a corporate culture at your workplace? What values are considered important there?
2. Take a look at your personal values about religion and politics. Where did they come from? Are they the same as the values of your parents or the people you were around as a child? Suggest some ideas about where your personal values came from.
3. Using Spranger's ideas about values, would you consider yourself a religious, theoretical, social, political, aesthetic, or economic person? Why do you think so?
4. Take the Rath Test to look at your own values. Are your true values the same as the beliefs you thought you held?
5. How does the mass media change or mold our values?

Multiple Choice

1. Robbie spends his free time with his family and friends. He values his relationships with others. According to Spranger's theory, what kind of person is he likely to be?
   a. Theoretical
   b. Social
   c. Political
   d. Aesthetic
2. The importance or worth we attach to different objects or issues in our lives is a definition of:
   a. Values
   b. Corporate culture

    c. Organizational values

    d. A value system

3. Which of the following is *not* true of organizational values?

    a. They evolve over time.

    b. They reflect what the company stands for.

    c. Workers or members will be judged by how well they fit the organizational values.

    d. Unhappiness at work has nothing to do with organizational values.

4. Rayanne strongly values environmental issues, but when she hears friends making jokes about environmentalists, she laughs along with them. According to the Rath Test, which of the questions would she have a hard time answering yes to?

    a. Is this value consistent throughout my life?

    b. Will I defend this value publicly?

    c. Do I like and respect this value?

    d. Have I considered the consequences of my choice?

5. Social scientists have found that most Americans value several things about their jobs, which include all of the following *except:*

    a. Valuing leisure time.

    b. Valuing the kind of work that they do.

    c. Valuing a good salary and benefits package.

    d. Valuing being treated in a humane and personalized way.

Case 5–1

Changing Values or Changing Jobs?

Bill has been working for the same small construction company for the past 20 years, after serving in the Navy. Most of the workers Bill's age have now retired or moved on and have been replaced by young guys just out of high school. The original owner has even retired, so his son is now the boss. When the original owner was in charge, company policy was strict about signing in and out of work, safety precautions, and keeping cigarettes and alcohol off of the construction site. Now, Bill gets the feeling that the company is more like a party every day for the younger workers. They come in late and leave early, don't wear hard hats if they don't feel like it, and smoke right on the job—they even drink beer during the lunch break. The new owner doesn't say anything—he even joins them now and then! And the young workers are bringing their friends in to fill new job openings, so there are more and more of these guys on the job all the time. Bill is very uncomfortable at work these days. He doesn't want to join them at breaks, and the other guys are giving him a lot of grief for being such a stick-in-the-mud. He's starting to dislike his job and has a real struggle to get there every day. He'd like to take early retirement but can't really afford to. He'd like to get another job, but he doesn't think it will be easy to find anything at his age. So now he's stuck.

1. How would you describe the organizational values or the corporate culture of the construction company?
2. Why is Bill so unhappy at work these days? Is there anything that he can do to feel more positive about his job?
3. With the information you have about Bill, which of Spranger's types does he fit in with best? What about the other workers on the job?

What Gets You Up in the Morning?

Lola and Teresita are changing beds in the hospital where they work. Lola says, "I don't know why I bother to come in every day. I'm not getting anything out of this job. The nursing supervisor treats us like we're incompetent, I barely make enough money to feed the kids, and the patients don't even thank us for the extra things we do for them," she sighs.

"Then why are you here? There must be something! What made you decide to go through all those years of school and hard work to be a nurse?" asks Teresita.

"Hmmm," says Lola thoughtfully, "Well, I guess there is something . . . I really get a lot of satisfaction knowing that I'm helping people, even when they're too sick to know what's going on. I guess it's those good feelings I get inside, like I've really accomplished something, that makes it all worthwhile. That's really motivating for me. I guess if I just keep that in mind, I can overlook the negatives. Thanks for reminding me!"

What gets you up in the morning? Think about that question for a minute: It's not really the alarm clock, the smell of coffee, the cat meowing to be let out, or the kids asking for breakfast. We get up in the morning because we are motivated to accomplish something every day. Every day, we find the energy to do what we want to do that day, whether it is making just enough money to make ends meet, working in the garden, saving lives in a hospital emergency room, caring for our family, or writing the great American novel. In this chapter, we will be talking about **motivation**—what gives us the desire to think about what we want or need in our lives, set goals, and work toward trying to meet those goals in order to get what we need.

THEORIES OF MOTIVATION

There are many well-known theories about motivation. We will be talking about only a few of them. As you read this chapter, think about how these theories fit with what motivates you in your own life.

Maslow's Hierarchy of Needs

Abraham Maslow, one of the most influential psychologists of the past few decades, said that we are motivated or driven to action by trying to meet all our needs. According to **Maslow's hierarchy of needs theory,** we have basic needs that must be met before we can move on to try to meet higher needs. Also, after a need has been met, it will not motivate us anymore.

Maslow presents five general categories of needs that we meet every day, and that we also work toward during our lives. We have to meet these needs in the right order, but some of us get stuck and don't move up through all five categories.[1] They are:

1. **Physiological needs,** such as food, water, and air.
2. **Safety needs,** such as shelter, whether it is in an abandoned car or a mansion in Beverly Hills.
3. **Love and belonging needs,** such as making friends, and identifying ourselves with a group.
4. **Self-esteem needs,** or achieving goals, feeling competent, and gaining the approval of other people.
5. **Self-actualization,** or reaching our full potential.

---

[1] Abraham Maslow, *Motivation and Personality* (New York: Harper & Row, 1970), pp. 46–65.

Think about these needs as you try to reach them every day. For example, it will be hard for you to concentrate on reading this chapter if you haven't eaten for a day or two (physiological needs), or if you are homeless and living in a dark alley (safety needs). The hierarchy of needs theory also works for long-term goals. For example, it may be hard for you to feel good about meeting a big deadline at work (self-esteem needs) if you have no co-workers, friends, or family (love and belonging needs) to share that good news with. If you don't feel self-actualized right now, don't worry—Maslow believed that it takes most of our lives to achieve self-actualization, and many of us don't get there at all.

McClelland's Needs Theory

Psychologist David McClelland explains another type of needs theory. In his **McClelland's needs theory,** we have needs for *power, achievement,* and *affiliation* (interacting with other people). We all have these three needs, but in different amounts.[2]

The **power needs** can be used in either a positive or negative way. Supervisors or managers won't be effective without this need, but when carried too far power may be used to control other people. People with a high need for power often choose careers, such as politics or psychiatry, where they can make decisions that affect other people's lives.

People with high **achievement needs** usually have high energy levels, like challenges, and like to get feedback about how they are doing. They may be competitive and may even enjoy conflicts or confrontations.

We all have social needs, or **affiliation needs.** For some people, this is strong enough to motivate them to go to work every day, where they will have other people to socialize with. This need also motivates us to join groups, stay in contact with our families, or go to parties. People with a high affiliation need often have a strong desire to be liked and accepted by others.

Think about your own needs in these three areas. For example, if you were to win the lottery and become an instant multimillionaire, what would you like to do? Some answers might include find-

[2] David C. McClelland, *Human Motivation* (Glenview, IL: Scott, Foresman, 1985).

ing a cure for AIDS (achievement needs), throwing a worldwide party (affiliation needs), or buying a small island to rule over (power needs).

Argyris's Maturity Theory

Chris Argyris, a motivation expert, has developed a theory based on the idea that all healthy, normal people develop through life from immaturity to maturity. According to **Argyris's maturity theory,** most adults are mature, but some workplace organizations don't treat them as if they are. Some workplaces don't allow people to use all their talents and abilities, or companies take away people's self-control and make them passive. When this happens, mature workers will be frustrated and unmotivated, while other workers will not be able to grow to maturity on the job. Employees will then either leave the job, stay and fight (through labor unions or informal work groups), or give up and adapt. **Workplace adapting** is the most common choice, and it is also the hardest on emotional and mental health.[3]

Have you been in a workplace situation where you are treated as though you are immature? This **immature treatment** makes most people receiving it feel resentful or powerless, and the result is they don't work very hard. Imagine a job where there is a powerful chain of command, you are tied closely to the leader, and you are unable to meet your inner needs. In that kind of situation, how motivated are you likely to be to work hard at your job?

McGregor's Theory X and Theory Y

Douglas **McGregor's Theory X and Theory** Y on attitudes also can be examined in terms of motivation. Theory X managers see people as not being motivated to work, but motivated to do other enjoyable things instead of working. Because of this, Theory X managers would say that people need to be motivated to work by being offered **extrinsic rewards,** or external rewards. These would include, for example, bonuses for good performance, profit-sharing plans, overtime pay, extra duty pay, impressive-sounding titles, pay raises, and nice office furnishings.

---

[3] Chris Argyris, *Personality and Organization* (New York: Harper & Row, 1957).

Theory Y managers see workers as enjoying their work and being motivated by the satisfaction of the work itself. According to Theory Y, then, we are motivated to work because of **intrinsic rewards,** or internal rewards. These would include, for example, satisfaction from increased responsibilities, opportunities for personal growth, the ability to participate in decision-making, the assignment of interesting and varied tasks, and having some freedom on the job.[4]

When you think about whether your own motivation to work fits more with Theory X or Theory Y, you may find that you work for both some of the extrinsic and some of the intrinsic rewards. Most people's immediate reaction to the question "Why do you work?" is "For the money!" Yet, in national surveys, about 90 percent of people say they would work even if they did not need the money. Would you? What do you get out of working?

Skinner's Behavior Modification Theory and Reinforcement Theory

Another giant in the field of psychology in recent decades was B. F. Skinner. Most of what we hear about behavior modification and positive reinforcement comes from his work. **Skinner's behavior modification and reinforcement theory** says that we are motivated to carry out or not to carry out behaviors based on the results that come from those behaviors. If the result of our action is a positive reward, we will be motivated to keep doing that action. If the result is no reward—or worse, if the result is a punishment—we will be motivated to stop doing that action. For the reinforcement to work, we have to be able to see the cause-and-effect relationship, and the reinforcement has to be something that we want or value.[5]

Think about how often positive reinforcement happens in your own life. If you receive performance bonuses at work, you will be more likely to repeat the kind of performance that earned you the bonus. If you want your children to start picking up their room or doing their homework, you may have discovered the power of praise or other rewards in getting those behaviors to

---

[4] Douglas McGregor, *The Human Side of Enterprise* (New York: McGraw-Hill), pp. 33–35.
[5] B. F. Skinner, *Beyond Freedom and Dignity* (New York: Alfred A. Knopf, 1971).

happen. If you want your dog to learn to sit, you feed it a doggie treat when the dog sits on command. But when nothing positive comes from our actions, we are not as likely to be motivated to repeat them.

Expectancy Theory

This theory of motivation brings together pieces of other theories. In general, the **expectancy theory** says that we can explain our behavior in terms of our goals and choices, and the expectation that our goals will be reached. To understand this theory, according to psychologist Victor Vroom, you need to understand its three parts: expectancy, instrumentality, and valence. **Expectancy** is a person's belief that if he or she tries hard enough, the result will be better performance. **Instrumentality** is how likely it is that something good or bad will come about as a result of the better performance. **Valence** is the value that an individual person places on the reward.[6]

Does expectancy theory explain your motivation, or lack of it, in certain circumstances? As an example, let's say you are in a pharmaceutical sales job where the reward for top salesperson during the month of January is a free weekend in Seattle. You believe that you are the best salesperson in the company and could easily win the trip. But if you don't have any desire to visit the rainy Pacific Northwest in the winter, then even though instrumentality and expectancy may be high, valence will be low, and you will not be motivated to sell much that month.

MOTIVATION AND SELF-ESTEEM

Did one of the theories described fit best with your own motivation to accomplish things in life? Regardless of which type of theory fits best, theorists agree that we are motivated best when our own self-concept and self-esteem are built up. This is an important idea to remember when you are trying to motivate others, too. For most of us, a carrot works better than a stick!

---

[6] Victor H. Vroom, *Work and Motivation* (New York: John Wiley & Sons, 1964), pp. 170–74.

Key Terms

motivation

Maslow's hierarchy of needs theory

physiological needs

safety needs

love and belonging needs

self-esteem needs

self-actualization

McClelland's needs theory

power needs

achievement needs

affiliation needs

Argyris's maturity theory

workplace adapting

immature treatment

McGregor's Theory X and Y

extrinsic rewards

intrinsic rewards

Skinner's behavior modification and reinforcement theory

expectancy theory

expectancy

instrumentality

valence

Review Questions

1. Thinking about McClelland's needs theory, would you consider yourself as someone with strong needs for power? achievement? affiliation? Why? Which of the three is your strongest need?
2. According to Argyris's maturity theory, are you treated as though you are mature in your workplace? Describe situations in which you or other workers are treated as if they are mature or immature.
3. Thinking about McGregor's Theory X and Theory Y, do you perform better in situations where you are motivated by intrinsic or by extrinsic rewards? Which do you think is a more powerful type of reward overall?
4. Think about situations in your life where you were rewarded and where you were punished after a behavior—whether it was lying to your mom as a child, or getting extra credit in school for extra work. Which type of outcome was more powerful in getting you to change your behavior? Describe the situation.

5. Think about Maslow's hierarchy of needs theory as it applies to your own life. Where would you place yourself on the hierarchy? Why? What could you do to move up?

Multiple Choice

1. Which of the following outcomes would make most people *more* likely to want to work late when the boss asks them to, according to Skinner's theory?
   a. They receive time-and-a-half overtime pay if they stay late.
   b. They get yelled at if they don't work late.
   c. They get moved to a smaller office if they don't stay late.
   d. They don't have to be in charge of the coffee fund any more if they agree to stay late.
2. The three parts of Vroom's expectancy theory include all of the following *except:*
   a. Expectancy
   b. Instrumentality
   c. Valence
   d. Salience
3. Russell's boss is a Theory X manager, according to McGregor's Theory X and Theory Y. Which of the following rewards would his boss be *most* likely to use in motivating employees?
   a. Promoting employee self-satisfaction.
   b. Giving employees opportunities for personal growth.
   c. Giving pay raises and bonuses for good performance.
   d. Assigning employees more interesting tasks.
4. According to Argyris's maturity theory, which situation would motivate employees to do a good job?
   a. Setting up a powerful chain of command above them.
   b. Allowing them to use their talents and abilities.
   c. Taking away their self-control.
   d. Making sure they are passive and tied closely to the manager or boss.
5. Samantha has a high energy level, likes competition, likes to get feedback about how she is doing, and enjoys challenging activities. According to McClelland's needs theory, she has a high need for:

a. Affiliation
b. Power
c. Achievement
d. Aggression

What Max and Molly Need

Luis Venegas teaches second grade at an elementary school in rural Washington State. His students come from a variety of backgrounds, from farm families to children of professionals. Most of his students are doing fine academically and socially, but Luis is concerned about two students who are struggling in school and don't seem to have any friends.

The first student, Molly, lives with her older sister and their dad on a small farm. Luis has noticed that Molly often comes to school in the same clothes she wore the day before, sometimes without a jacket on cold days, and she often looks like she needs a bath. It's lucky for Molly that the school has a breakfast and lunch program, because Luis suspects that these may be the only meals she eats regularly.

The second student, Max, lives with his parents and two younger brothers in town. His parents are very busy building up a real estate business in the area. They see a lot of clients at night and on weekends, and are busy in the office when they're not showing houses. Max looks clean, well fed, and well taken care of, but to Luis he seems very lonely. He clings to Luis much more than the other children in class, he often asks if Luis likes him, and he makes remarks about not being good enough to play with the other kids in class or do well in school. "I've got to think of a plan to help these two kids succeed here," thinks Luis; "hmmm, I wonder what Maslow would have to say about them?"

1. What would Abraham Maslow say about Molly's and Max's needs, according to Maslow's hierarchy of needs theory? What are their needs right now?

2. What could Luis do to help Molly succeed in school, based on what her needs are right now? What about Max?

3. Why are the other kids in class succeeding, based on Maslow's theory? Where would you place their needs?

The Number One Innovator— You!

"How does Kim always seem to come up with great ideas like that," one of his co-workers asked another after a staff meeting. "I don't know," the other replied, "but I couldn't think up things like that if you gave me five years, let alone five minutes." "I guess some of us just have it and the rest of us don't," mused her friend.

Kim had triumphed again with a creative plan for his company, and more fuel had been added to the belief that creativity is something that only the gifted few possess. Nothing could be further from the truth. All of us are creative; we simply need to find ways to unleash that creativity and express it.

INNOVATION AND HUMAN RELATIONS

What does innovation—or the lack of it—have to do with human relations? Everyone has a deep well of creativity. If it hasn't been used, social and interpersonal factors are quite possibly a part of the reason. Perhaps you were the child whose parents were forever warning you to be "careful" and not to be messy or do crazy things. Creativity, the ability to come up with new, fresh ideas, requires a little carelessness, a lot of messiness, and—yes—some genuine craziness at times.

Perhaps you have a boss who rejects any new idea with **"killer phrases"** such as "we've tried it before," "it'll cost too much," or "it won't work." Or maybe you're that boss; we hope not. The point is that the workplace often continues the **creativity-killing environments** of many childhoods.

Today more than ever we need to be creative. Our society rewards creativity only after the mold has been broken, after the new product has been accepted and proven, and after the cynics have been proven wrong. The trick is to get past that set of "don'ts" that other people erect. The following steps should help in that process:

1. **Begin to think of yourself as a creative person.** Many times students have come to us with the plea, "I couldn't create anything new and original if my life depended on it." Our response usually is to agree. "Yes," we reply, "You're right, and the reason you're right is precisely because you believe that you are not creative. You seem to believe that with all of your heart. Thus, your first step is to attack that very belief; it's the only thing that is standing in your way." Notice that, once again, low self-esteem is the chief culprit. Happily, just as a belief that you aren't creative can hurt you, the opposite belief can help you on your way to a more creative existence.

2. **Learn to operate in the "open mode."** As we go about our daily lives, we operate mostly in the "closed mode." The **closed mode** contains elements of anxiety, pressure (including pressure to conform to others), stress, and little humor. The **open mode,** on the other hand, is relaxed, laid-back, less focused, and less purposeful. Getting into and staying in the open mode requires us to change our attitudes toward time. Our usual workplace attitude toward time is itself one of the greatest killers of creativity.

One caution: There are times, especially at work, when we need to be in the closed mode. At such times, we need to be focused, time-conscious, and purposeful. Becoming creative involves getting to the point where we can control the mode we are in when it needs to be changed.

3. **Begin to view problems as opportunities.** Many creative ideas started out as problems. The people who solved them did so because they saw the problem as an opportunity to think of a creative

solution. Mostly, we are suggesting an attitude change (see chapters 3 and 4). The attitude of fear that confronts many of us when a problem arises spells defeat because it creates a barrier to innovation.

4. Don't be afraid to break the rules.   Other words also can substitute for "rules" here: traditions, habits, ordinary procedures, and so forth. To increase our creativity, we need to step outside the traditional ways of approaching problems and go beyond the limits set by the past.

The **nine-dot puzzle** is often used as an example of our respect for rules. Participants are instructed to connect nine dots using only four straight lines, without lifting the pencil or pen from the paper.

See if you can do it. Check your solution with the one at the end of this chapter. Hint: Think about the rules, or boundaries, suggested by the nine dots; then think in terms of going beyond those limits. The gimmick is that most people trying this puzzle think of the nine dots as forming a square. Their second assumption is that going outside of that square would be breaking the rules. If you still haven't solved the puzzle, use this final clue to do so. Many of the "rules" in our lives are like the nine-dot puzzle: They keep us from getting original thoughts only if we let them.

5. Look for the "second right answer."   Another major limitation to our creative abilities is our tendency to think of an idea that seems reasonable, and then to run with it, ignoring the many other possibilities that often exist. Outside of math and some areas of science, several "right" answers might be possible. Usually, some of these are a lot better than others. So, don't stop with the **second right answer;** go on to the third, the fourth, as far as you can go in the time you have.

For example, Harry is trying to figure out what to do about the budget cuts in his company. He chairs the finance committee, to which he will be giving recommendations tomorrow. He has decided to cut back production and is planning to ask the committee for suggestions about implementing the cutbacks. The problem: He is ignoring dozens of cost-cutting measures that might allow the current level of production to continue. He's also ignoring the introduction of a new product that promises to greatly increase sales. Worst of all, he is cutting off the committee members from making creative suggestions, except for cutbacks. What he needs is to hear a "second right answer."

6. **Don't be afraid to make mistakes.**   Some of us want to hide our mistakes, and to do everything concisely and carefully to avoid being wrong. A creative decision maker has to be willing to take risks, and taking risks involves the very real possibility that you will make mistakes. But, making mistakes is one of the most effective ways of learning. The president of a successful, fast-growing computer company tells his employees, "We're doing things nobody has ever done before. Therefore, we are going to be making mistakes. My advice to you: Make your mistakes, but make them in a hurry."

7. **Learn to "play the violin."**   Someone once asked management expert Peter Drucker the secret of becoming a good manager. His answer was **"Learn to play the violin."** Of course, he didn't mean that becoming a violinist would help directly. He meant that anyone will make better—and more creative—decisions when he or she has stepped outside the ordinary context of life into one with different values and perspectives. You are likely to become more creative once you have stepped outside your comfort zone.

8. **Turn your ideas into actions.**   Finally, once you have increased your creative output, don't stop there. How many good ideas have you had that were used later with great success by someone else? No matter how good an idea is, it won't do anything effective unless it is put into action. Implement your creativity!

INCREASING CREATIVITY IN THE WORKPLACE

What steps can be taken to improve the creative quality of workers? Probably the most important point of attack is the workplace environment. Learn to recognize your workplace environment in terms of how much creativity it allows and encourages. In some wonderful workplaces, employees are encouraged to come up with creative ways to save money, to increase worker safety, or to increase productivity. Often, a monetary reward is offered. In other workplaces, creativity is discouraged. Doing things the "same old way" is encouraged—nearly worshipped.

If you are a manager, you can do a great deal to make sure that your workplace is one of creativity encouragement. First, make the work rewarding and fulfilling as much as possible. Obviously, some tasks are more interesting than others, and some seem harder to make interesting than others. Second, use positive reinforcement to encourage creative ideas. Positive reinforcement includes positive statements, monetary rewards, nonverbal encouragement—anything that rewards positive effort with positive results.

If you are a worker, begin by evaluating you own work environment. Then ask yourself, "What can I do to allow myself and others to become more innovative on this job?" If your evaluation of the work environment and answers to the question are negative, perhaps you should find a job that will reward and stimulate your creativity.

Creativity is important both to you and to your workplace. It requires getting away from the "normal" ways of seeing the world. Creative work fulfills us in ways nothing else can, and it's a wonderful tool for motivation and staying interested in your work. It is important to human relations because creativity rarely happens in a vacuum; it is encouraged and discouraged by others in your environment. Besides, creativity is fun!

Key Terms

innovation

creativity

"killer phrases"

creativity-killing
environments

closed mode

open mode

nine-dot puzzle

second right

answer

"Learn to play the
violin"

Review Questions

1. Why is creativity in the workplace such an important issue?
2. In your opinion, why is workplace so often the last place you ever find creativity?
3. List and explain each of the eight steps you can take to improve your own creativity.
4. What does it mean to be in the "open mode"? How can the open mode allow for greater creativity?
5. What is meant by "the second right answer?" Explain.

Multiple Choice

1. Which of the following statements about creativity is *correct?*
   a. Creativity has to do with the section of the country you grew up in.
   b. A creative person will always have a high IQ.
   c. Creativity has a great deal to do with perception.
   d. Most people can never become creative, because of noncreative genes.
2. Which of the following is *true* of "the second right answer"?
   a. The "second right answer" is a logical fallacy. Questions usually have only one right answer; to go beyond that creates confusion and contradictions.
   b. The "second right answer" is a fallacy that sees either one side or the other of an argument as correct; no compromise is used, which is wrong.
   c. The "second right answer" aids creativity by forcing us out of settling for the "right answer" that first occurs to us.
   d. The "second right answer" is the answer that comes from an opponent in a formal debate. It is to be argued and defeated.
3. Thinking of yourself as a creative person will:
   a. Be of no help to you in increasing creativity. You are either creative or you're not. No amount of positive thinking will change that.
   b. Be of great help to you in increasing creativity. You are often just as creative as you believe you are. Positive thinking can increase creativity.

    c. Deceive other people into thinking you are creative and thus might help you obtain work in creative occupations.

    d. Simply frustrate your creative challenges.

4. The nine-dot puzzle is often used as an example of what killer of creativity, especially in the workplace?

    a. Our respect for following rules.

    b. The authority of a negative manager.

    c. Negative thinking.

    d. Our inborn love of geometry.

5. Which of the following statements about the "open mode" is *false?*

    a. People are usually more creative when they are in the open mode.

    b. It is relaxed, expansive, and less purposeful.

    c. It should always be avoided in the workplace.

    d. Operating in it often involves giving yourself sufficient time.

Case 7–1

The Creativity Killer

Rhonda Elwood worked for Yaldor, Inc., a young advertising agency in a small Indiana town. For the past three years, Yaldor won local awards for the quality of its material, especially radio and TV spots for small stations. Rhonda was only an "ad assistant." In her second year with the firm, she felt that Yaldor should give her some projects where she could be the creative director.

Near the end of every fiscal year, the planning process would begin for the next year's accounts. Rhonda's team leader, Gary Younger, urged everyone to come up with new ideas. "Let's be as creative as possible. We all know that there are limitless ideas out there, if we can just tap into them." Rhonda and her friend Betty were sitting together in the planning meeting. Rhonda whispered, "Yeah, as though he really means it! My ideas have about as much value as those from somebody off the street," she complained.

Younger ran a lively brainstorming session, though with very little participation from Rhonda and Betty. After the meeting, he approached the pair and asked them into his office.

Younger: So, what's wrong with you two? You're always right there when I ask you to do something new. What's different this time?

Rhonda: Well, remember the three spots for Axel Dry Cleaners we cooked up several months ago?

Younger: Yeah, you mean the one Mr. Normington killed?

Betty: That's our point exactly! He's been running the place for six months, and during that time he's rejected every new idea we've come up with. Worse yet, we know for a fact that he doesn't even take the time to look at a lot of our stuff that gets to his office.

Rhonda: So now you're asking us to help brainstorm for new ideas. Sorry, but they just won't materialize. Of course, say we did come up with some great ideas. If Normington found out who thought of them, they'd be out the window in a hurry.

Younger: Are you sure you're not getting a little paranoid about this?

Rhonda: Well, maybe we are, but who could blame us?

Younger: I'll have a word with Mr. Normington. Meantime, please try not to let your attitudes ruin your positive work in this agency.

1. What should Younger say in his meeting with Mr. Normington? Why?

2. Can you think of some strategies Gary Younger could use to stimulate some creative thinking from Rhonda and Betty? Explain.

3. Put yourself in Rhonda's and Betty's place. What steps could they take to change their attitudes and become more creative?

Solution to nine-dot puzzle:

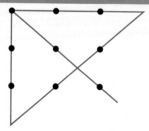

8

Learning to Deal with Change in Your Own Life

Jeanne was a model employee in her company. She was as efficient as she was personable and helpful. Twice she had received the employee-of-the-month award. Then her 10-year marriage broke up. Her former husband moved to another state, leaving her alone with two young children. Though she tried very hard not to let the radical changes in her personal life affect her performance at work, she found herself not being as effective as she was before. Lately, others had started to notice. Alone at night she pondered, "What can I do? I need to get hold of myself."

During our working lives, most of us experience some type of major personal change. The better we understand the effects of such changes on our lives, the better we can cope—and the sooner we can return to normal work performance.

SEVEN CATEGORIES OF CHANGE

Change is one of the most important producers of stress. The stress comes mostly from the tremendous sense of loss that usually accompanies any major change. Although even small changes can be difficult to deal with, we are primarily looking here at the important dramatic changes that take place in a person's life. They can be put into seven categories:[1]

1. Loss.
2. Separation.
3. Relocation.
4. A change in a relationship with someone important.
5. A change in direction.
6. A change in health.
7. Personal growth.

These seven kinds of change are all tough to deal with. They also have several other points in common:

- **They happen to all of us.**   Although these events aren't a regular part of all of our lives, they are things that are likely to happen at least a few times. These changes are simply a part of being alive.

- **Most of them happen without our wanting them to.** Changes that seem to be beyond our control are the toughest ones to deal with. Eric Margenau, a psychologist who deals with the effects of change, says, "From a stress standpoint, you're better off making a choice and having it turn out to be a wrong choice than to have the choice made for you, even if it's right."[2] If we had our choice, we would choose not to have most of these changes happen to us.

- **Each one of these changes has its own "babies."**   Any time big changes take place, they create other changes as by-products. These are called the "babies" of change. For example, a death in the family changes attitudes toward others besides the person who has died, toward oneself, and toward the work one does. Sometimes the biggest problems come from the "babies" of a major change.

- **These changes affect us before, during, after the actual**

---

[1] Shad Helmstetter, *You Can Excel in Times of Change* (New York: Simon & Schuster, 1991), pp. 22–23.
[2] Quoted in Sharon Faelten, *Take Control of Your Life: A Complete Guide to Stress Relief* (Emmaus, PA: Rodale Press, 1988), p. 119.

change.   Often we have warnings of major changes. The anxiety from those warnings is often more intense than the change itself when it finally comes. The during and after stages are obvious. The most intense stage is after the change—especially when that change involves an ending of some significant part of our lives.

THE SIX STAGES OF PERSONAL CHANGE

Figure 8–1 shows the process of healthy reaction to personal change. An emotionally healthy person will go through all of these steps, although the time spent in each of them will vary. If you fail to go through each of these steps, you will be missing an important part of the mending process. If you skip one, you will likely have to go back to it later.

1. Emotional standstill. The first reaction we usually have to a major change is shock. "Oh no," we'll say, "How did it happen? When?" In shock there is a gap between rational thinking and emo-

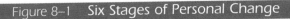

Figure 8–1   Six Stages of Personal Change

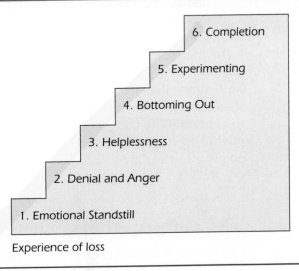

6. Completion

5. Experimenting

4. Bottoming Out

3. Helplessness

2. Denial and Anger

1. Emotional Standstill

Experience of loss

tions.[3] Even when the change is expected, such as a death after a long illness or a divorce, both husband and wife knew was going to happen, the shock element is there. We might be mentally prepared for the change, but intense emotional reactions are still likely to happen.

2. Denial and anger. When faced with a major tragedy, people often say, "I just don't believe it!" Although many of us will accept in our minds what has happened, we will continue to deny it with our emotions. Ideally, this denial period will be over in a few weeks or months. The longer the period lasts, the longer it will take to move through the healing process.[4]

Sometimes, the denial will be replaced by anger. The anger felt at this time usually contains a feeling of helplessness—of being a victim who was unable to prevent the change. Most psychologists advise that this anger should be expressed in a way that will not harm others.

3. Helplessness.   At the helpless step in this process, we are still suffering from the "ending" that has taken place. We are often afraid to "bottom out" because despair is the result. Most people will do many things to avoid the feeling of despair. Thus, we will usually make one of two mistakes; either we will try to share our emotions with too many other people or we will retreat into isolation. Both extremes are destructive. The first one is a quick way to lose friends, and the second is self-defeating.[5]

4. Bottoming out.   For the first time since the event, you find yourself able to "let go" of the emotional burden which has been weighing you down. Often a person knows when this bottom point has been reached by a peaceful feeling that comes one morning. More often, the step is gradual. Bottoming out means releasing the thoughts, tensions, memories, and emotions that have allowed you to hold onto the past. At this point, you are allowing the life-completing processes to take their course. The shock, the denial, and the anger are becoming memories.[6]

---

[3] Bernadine Kreis and Alice Pattie, *Up From Grief: Patterns of Recovery* (New York: Seabury Press, 1969), pp. 11–23.

[4] Gail Sheehy, *Pathfinders: Overcoming the Crises of Adult Life and Finding Your Own Path to Well-Being* (New York: William Morrow, 1981), pp. 313–14.

[5] See Bernadine Kreis and Alice Pattie, p. 36.

[6] L. John Mason, *Stress Passages: Surviving Life's Transitions Gracefully* (Berkeley, CA: Celestial Arts, 1988), pp. 230–32.

5. Experimenting.   Now that you have bottomed out, and are on your way to recovery, your normal curiosities and desires to experiment are coming back to life. If the event was a divorce or death of a spouse, this is the point where spending time with the opposite sex with romantic intentions will become a possibility. If the major change was loss of a job, your experimentation will be with tasks and opportunities that you probably wouldn't have considered before. You now have emotions left over for other people and other projects. Less of your energy is now being consumed by your own recovery. For this reason, you are likely to be good company for others. Notice also that we are often forced into another job—out of financial necessity—before we are emotionally ready to adapt. In such a case, the "bottoming out" and "experimenting" must be done in different contexts.

6. Completion.   Some people call this step "rebirth." Although that term might sound a bit overdramatic, it is accurate. The cycle you have gone through is complete. This does not mean that you won't ever again be haunted by the past, nor does it mean there won't be days when you feel you've gone right back to one of the earlier steps. That sort of occasional *regression* is also normal. But now you have a new perspective. Far from being blocked out, the event has become a part of your active memory, a part which you can think about without undue pain.

CHANGE AND SELF-ESTEEM

What we have just described is a natural process, but the sufferers still maintain control of their destiny. Going through the steps does require some effort, but millions of people who have never read this book have come through the process beautifully. Knowing each step, though, will help you see that your emotional recovery is both important and normal.

The effects of personal change often are related to our self-esteem. Any change that affects something or someone close to us is likely to upset our view of who we are—the self-concept. Anything that affects self-concept also touches our self-esteem. Divorce is a good example of a change that may cause us to question who we are. The process of healing involves getting back to a point where we know who we are and where we feel good about ourselves.

Here are some hints that will help you when you encounter an important change in your own life.[7]

- **Recognize and understand the change.** Be sure that the change is what you think it is. For example, when your boss retires, you might assume that the situation at work will be hopeless when maybe it will be better.

- **Make the decision to accept or reject the change.** When you include changes over which you might have some control, this is an important decision. When you have no control over the change, it's still a good idea to think in terms of acceptance. The six stages of personal change have to do with accepting the change and allowing it to become a useful part of your life.

- **Choose the attitude to have toward the change.** We often make the mistake of thinking of ourselves as victims who are unable to form our own attitudes when outside forces affect us. Remember that the choice of attitude is yours, and yours alone.

- **Choose the style use in dealing with the change.** Some are giving in, partnering with someone else, passively or actively resisting, retreating, and actively accepting.

- **Choose the action to take *every day*.** Part of dealing with change—and with anything else that threatens to upset your life—is to live one day at a time. Each day is a new attack, a new plan. Make sure that each day represents a renewed effort.

- **Review the steps and evaluate your progress every day.** The best way to make a renewed effort is to make a daily progress check. You have an advantage over people who haven't seen this book. With some idea of where you're headed, the progress you make can be both faster and more effective.

Personal change is a reality we all live with in the 1990s. Learning how to cope with it when it happens can help you when changes

---

[7] These six steps are based on Helmstetter, pp. 145–80.

affect your life directly, and can also help you understand other people who are touched by extreme change. This knowledge will help your human relations greatly.

Key Terms

The seven categories of change:

1. Loss.
2. Separation.
3. Relocation.
4. A change in a relationship with someone important.
5. A change in direction.
6. A change in health.
7. Personal growth

"babies" of change

The six stages of personal change:

1. Emotional standstill
2. Denial and anger
3. Helplessness
4. Bottoming out
5. Experimenting
6. Completion

Review Questions

1. Someone once said that recognizing the need for change is the most difficult step in the change process. Why might that be true? Explain.
2. List and explain each of the six steps of personal change management. Why are they all essential?
3. Pretend you are a manager with an employee who is going through a painful divorce that is affecting the quality of his job perfomance. How could the material in this chapter be helpful to you?
4. List at least three hints that should be helpful to you when you encounter an important change in your own life.
5. What is meant by the concept of "babies" of change?

Multiple Choice

1. Which of the following is *not* an example of an intense personal life change?
   a. Death of a spouse.
   b. Loss of an important job.

c. An organizational development project.

d. A divorce.

2. Which of these statements about the seven major life changes is *false?*

a. They are all self-induced; that is, we are always to blame for them.

b. They happen to all of us.

c. Each one has its own "babies."

d. We feel the results of these changes before, during, and after the event.

3. John Carlyle skipped a step or two of the six stages of personal change when he lost his father in an auto accident. At times, he finds himself going back to the very beginning of the grieving process. What he is experiencing is called:

a. Dual personality

b. Déjà vu

c. Regression

d. Catatonia

4. At which step of the six stages of personal change should a divorced person begin to experiment with dating, assuming he or she does so?

a. Denial and anger

b. Bottoming out

c. Experimenting

d. Helplessness

5. The step in the six stages of change that can be called "trying but still failing" is known as . . .

a. denial and anger

b. bottoming out

c. experimenting

d. helplessness

**Case
8–1**

Goodbye, New England

Today was the big day for Mona Smith. She and her husband Mike had been talking about her possible transfer from Boston, Massachusetts, to Portland, Oregon. Today it became official. Mona already knew what she would do as soon as she got off work. On the way home, she would buy a bottle of the most expensive champagne she could find and surprise Mike with it. She had finally been offered her dream job. She would head the office of a large insurance company with a salary nearly twice that of her present one. "Mike is going to be overjoyed," she said to herself.

The celebration was all Mona had hoped. Mike was excited, just as she had predicted. But after the champagne was gone, the couple sat down to a serious discussion about their future. Mike was the first to admit that he was scared. "Moving almost 3,000 miles across the country is a big step," he admitted. "Gosh, I've never been west of Chicago. I've heard stories, but I have no idea what living in Portland will really be like." "Well," admitted his wife, "I'm frightened, too, if that helps any. But just think how well off we'll be, and how exciting the whole move really is."

Lying in bed later that night, both Mona and Mike Smith were thinking private thoughts. "Just think," Mike mused to himself, "I'll never see that gang I work with again. They're really okay. I'll miss 'em. I wonder if I'll even like the people in Oregon." Meantime, Mona was thinking, "Whew, I wonder if I'm really up to the job of being the manager of a corporate branch, even here in New England, let alone one in a part of the country I've never seen."

1. Many changes are about to take place in the lives of Mona, Mike, and their friends. Identify each of the changes and estimate the impact of each.

2. What steps can Mona and Mike take to lessen the stress of this major change in both of their lives?

3. Many of the personal change factors dealt with in this chapter have been negative events, such as death and divorce. How similar are the implications of pleasant changes such that facing Mona and Mike? Explain.

9 Chapter

Are You Stressed Out?

While you are standing in the checkout line at a sporting goods store, you overhear three friends talking among themselves.

Hiro: I'm so stressed out! I've been working overtime almost every day for the past three weeks!

Ron: That's nothing! Talk about stress. Ever since my wife started school last fall, I have had to take care of the kids while she's studying, and cook dinner every night after work!

Roberto: Well, there's no stress in *my* life! In the past year, I got married, moved 120 miles to live with my new wife, and started a new job here. Those are all *good* things!

Which of the situations do you think is the most stressful? It might surprise you to hear that most psychologists and health professionals would say that Roberto is the most stressed. Why? Because he has had several major changes in his life recently, and **stress** is defined as the body's response to any changes or demands made on it.

Our bodies can't tell the difference between stress from pleasant events, called **eustress** (holidays, sports events) and stress from unpleasant sources, called **distress** (getting divorced, losing a job). The effects on our bodies are the same, no matter what the cause of the stress. We need to have some stress in our lives. Without any stress—that is, without any changes or challenges—we would eventually die. Then why do we always think of stress as bad? It's bad because the eventual result of too much stress is exhaustion and a weakened immune system. Too much stress can lead to what are called stress-related illnesses: heart attacks, strokes, and ulcers. Stress is also suspected to play a part in other diseases, such as asthma, skin diseases (hives or eczema), allergies, colitis, migraine headaches, and cancer. To put it simply, stress can make us sick!

WHAT CAUSES STRESS?

Stressors, or the situations and events that cause stress, can come from many sources: frustration, inner conflict, daily hassles, major life changes, and our own irrational belief systems, to name a few. **Frustration** occurs when we are blocked from a goal we are seeking. **Inner conflict** occurs when we have to choose between alternatives. The alternatives can have a number of different outcomes:

- Two desirable outcomes—an **approach-approach conflict,** such as choosing between a banana split or a hot fudge sundae.
- Two undesirable outcomes—an **avoid-avoid conflict,** such as parking legally several blocks from where you're going or parking illegally much closer and getting a ticket.
- An outcome that has both good and bad effects—an **approach-avoid conflict,** such as eating a pizza but gaining extra pounds by doing so.

Daily hassles are those little annoyances we all face: oversleeping and being late for work, getting stuck in traffic, spilling food on a clean shirt, losing our keys, or burning the toast in the morning. Too many of these annoyances can cause stress. **Major life changes,** such as a friend's death, starting or stopping school, having a baby, being arrested, or getting married, can also cause stress. Major life changes and daily hassles can work together, too. For example, getting a divorce (a major life change) can create many little hassles, such as finding a place to live, doing the housework yourself, explaining the situation over and over to friends, and so on.

HOW TO LESSEN THE CAUSES OF STRESS

Some sources of stress are beyond our control, but some stress we create ourselves. In the rest of this chapter, we'll focus on ways to lessen the stress that we create within ourselves, and ways to reduce the damaging effects of too much stress.

1. **Change our belief systems.**   Since a source of stress can be our own belief systems, we need to learn to replace any **irrational beliefs** with more rational ones. Irrational beliefs include believing, for example, that everyone must love us and that we must be perfect. These beliefs can be blown out of proportion and create stress. By substituting more rational beliefs, such as believing that everyone makes mistakes sometimes and nobody is perfect, we can reduce the stress we create within ourselves.

2. **Take charge of our own lives.**   Learn to see problems as challenges to overcome, not as insurmountable obstacles. Find something important in your own life to make a commitment to: family, church, community, work, or a political cause. Confront stressors. Believe that you are in control and can change the outcome of stressful events.

3. **Find the humor in situations.**   Laughing at a stressful situation can make you feel better because you can't feel stress and humor at the same time. Humor is healthy because it relaxes us, which reduces stress.

4. **Compare ourselves to others in the same situation.**   If we see others in the same situation who are worse off, we can stop **creating catastrophes** of each one of our own situations, no matter how serious or trivial they really are. Seeing others who are overcoming a stressful situation should give us encouragement about our own problem.

5. **Take advantage of motivating stress.**   We need to have some challenges in our lives. Without any stress, we would be bored, unchallenged, unmotivated, and unproductive. Pay attention to what your most productive level of stress is, so that you can be at your best. For example, knowing that you are facing a deadline at work can give you the positive energy you need to get the project done on time.

6. **Learn to live with the stress we can't avoid.**   This doesn't mean to give in and give up, it means to accept the things we cannot

change. Accept the fact that some stressors are unavoidable and learn to think about them in a different way. For example, we may not be able to avoid traffic, but we can think of it in a different way; for example, as a time to listen to books on tape that we haven't found time to read.

TAKE CARE OF YOURSELF!

Because too much stress can weaken our immune systems, we can reduce the negative effects of stress by taking care of ourselves and making sure we stay healthy. To be as fit as possible, we have to change our health-related behaviors, not just when we feel stressed but on a regular schedule. Then, during the times we do feel stressed out, we will be healthier and better equipped to fight it.

1. **Relax!** Since it's impossible to be relaxed and stressed at the same time, relaxation techniques can reduce stress, at least temporarily. Some of these techniques include deep breathing, meditation, and biofeedback. Another is progressive relaxation, in which you close your eyes, focus on one muscle group at time, tighten and then relax it, and continue until all the muscle groups in your body are relaxed. Try it!

2. **Stay fit!** Eat balanced and nutritious meals on a regular schedule. Eat less fat and more fiber. Exercise at least twice a week for 20 minutes a day. If you are overweight, follow a weight-loss plan. Cut down on or cut out the use of alcohol and tobacco. Take care of yourself at work. For example, if you work in a place where you are exposed to high noise or chemicals, use earplugs or face masks. Avoid too much exposure to the sun.

3. **Have fun!** Build time into your schedule for rest and leisure. Get enough sleep every night. You need it to stay healthy! If you're saying to yourself you don't have time for fun, then you probably are in urgent need of some regular rest and leisure activity. Getting away from work or other stressful situations and doing something you enjoy makes you better able to handle stress later.

4. **Make friends!** Social support is important for relieving stress. Family and friends, or even a support group, can be good sources of emotional support when we're feeling low or feeling overwhelmed. We all could use help at one time or another, even if it's just a sympathetic ear.

5. **Reduce stress at work!** Find out what resources are offered

through your workplace. Many companies offer counseling: psychological, substance abuse, weight control, and so on. Some companies even offer services to reduce employee stress and the pressure of time, such as on-site day care, health and fitness clubs, and flexible work schedules.

6. **Manage your time and stop procrastinating!** One of the best ways to reduce stressed-out feelings is to get organized and plan your time so that you don't feel overwhelmed. **Time management** helps you to feel that you are in control and to plan what to expect. By managing your time, you can stop wasting available time and stop planning too many things for one time slot.

Keep a daily time plan and stick to it. Build in a cushion of time for emergencies. Build in time for leisure activities or for little rewards. Tinker with the schedule until it works—and then stick to it! One of the biggest problems in time management is *procrastination*. How can we stop putting things off until the last minute? Once you've made a time management plan, get started at the time you've planned. Break big tasks into small, manageable steps. Think positively. When the project is something you're anxious about, don't tell yourself that you're a failure; try telling yourself how good it will feel when you're finished. And give yourself some credit for work you have finished along the way!

Remember, stress is a part of all of our lives. If we don't control stress, it can have damaging effects on our health and well-being. We can learn to recognize sources of stress that we create within ourselves and to reduce this stress. We can also change our behaviors to increase our overall health, so that we are better able to handle stress.

 ## Key Terms

stress	approach-approach conflict	major life changes
eustress		irrational beliefs
distress	avoid-avoid conflict	creating catastrophes
frustration		social support
inner conflict	approach-avoid conflict	time management
	daily hassles	

Review Questions

1. Think about some major life changes you may have gone through recently. Did your stress level rise during that time? What daily hassles were associated with the major life changes?
2. How do you relax when faced with a stressor? If your relaxation strategies are unhealthy (drinking, smoking, or eating too much), what are you willing to substitute in place of your regular activities?
3. Thinking about the three types of inner conflict (approach-avoid, avoid-avoid, approach-approach), describe a conflict you have faced recently that fit with one of these types of conflict.
4. Why is stress considered a necessary part of life? When is stress a good thing?
5. Some people have criticized the suggestion that we "learn to live with the stress we can't avoid," saying that this suggestion sounds a lot like "copping-out." Explain why this suggestion is not meant as a cop-out.

Multiple Choice

1. Stress is defined as:
   a. Tension.
   b. Strain of overwork.
   c. A body's response to any changes or demands made on it.
   d. Pressure to fulfill an obligation.
2. Without any stress in our lives, we would:
   a. Eventually die.
   b. Achieve many more goals.
   c. Live longer, healthier lives.
   d. Spend less time shopping.
3. Stress is believed to contribute to which of these groups of illnesses:
   a. Allergies, strokes and migraine headaches.
   b. Heart attacks, cancer and skin disease.
   c. Hives, colitis and ulcers.
   d. All of the above.
4. Which of the following is *not* a way of lessening stress in our own lives?

1/2 line long

  a. Changing our belief systems.
  b. Finding the humor in situations.
  c. Managing time better.
  d. Creating more insignificant daily hassles.
 5. Inner conflict occurs when:
  a. We are blocked from a goal.
  b. We become sick from stress.
  c. We have to choose between alternatives.
  d. Pleasant stressors are presented.

Case 9–1

Too Much to DO!

Jade was close to tears after she got off the phone with her boss. Jade's roommate, Nicki, rushed over to her, with concern showing on her face.

Nicki: What's wrong, Jade? You look like you just lost your job or something!

Jade: I didn't lose it, but I'm going to quit if this keeps up! Ever since the company downsized last fall, I've been doing the work of three people! I work late every night, I bring work home on weekends, I'm going to fail that continuing education course I was taking because I can't keep up with it—and now my boss wants me to fly up to Portland for a conference this weekend and give a presentation—which he expects me to write in the next four days! I can't handle this anymore! I'm not eating, I'm living on coffee and cigarettes, and the only way I can get to sleep at night is with a couple of beers! I haven't gone to my aerobics class in months! I'm falling apart!

Nicki: Calm down Jade, you're just making yourself more stressed. It doesn't sound like you can get rid of your extra work load right this minute, but I'll bet you could be handling it a lot better than you are. Let's sit down and talk strategy.

Jade: I can't afford to set aside time for that!

Nicki: You can't afford *not* to! Now sit down.

1/2 line long

1. Why does Nicki say that Jade can't afford not to plan strategy for handling her stress?

2. What could Jade change in her personal life to reduce the level of stress she is feeling?

3. Is there anything Jade could change at work that could reduce her stress level?

10

Are You Always Ethical?

Katy was in her second year as a buyer for a large department store. One day, a pleasant-looking man walked into her office and handed her a sealed envelope. After identifying himself as representing a manufacturer from whom Katy had never bought, he slyly suggested that Katy open the envelope at home when she was alone. He left an order list from his company on her desk and walked out, promising to "call back in a few days." When Katy opened the envelope, she found 10 crisp 50-dollar bills. There would be no way of tracing this money or proving it came from its source. What should she do? What would you do?

Ethics has become a major issue in today's world, and for very good reasons. An unethical society—or workplace—hurts everyone involved. When we are all ethical and fair in our deals with one another, we all profit. The old saying, "What goes around comes around," is certainly true of ethical behavior.

The term **ethics** refers to the standards of conduct and morals in a particular society, based on the past and still respected in the present. **Morality**, on the other hand, deals more with how our behavior should conform to cultural—or even absolute—standards of behavior. Ethics is often more exact and is frequently based on a list of written guidelines.

TESTING YOUR ETHICS

Before deciding what to do, Katy could use one of several ethics tests to decide whether accepting the money would be ethical. First, she could use the **Golden Rule.** (Do to others as you would have them do to you.) To apply this rule, you would have to try it with every person and group of people affected by your decision. What if you were a stockholder in a competing company, for example. Would you want someone to compete with you on the basis of bribery?

Another useful ethical test is the **categorical imperative,** in which one asks, "What would the world be like if everyone did this, or felt it was OK to do this?" If Katy should ask this question, she could easily picture a world of bribery and deceit where competition based on high quality and service mean little or nothing. It would be a rotten world in many ways.

If she were to use the **principle of utilitarianism** as a test, Katy would ask, "What will do the most good for the largest number of people?" Taking the bribe would help Katy only in the short run and, perhaps, help the briber. In the long run, the manufacturing company might lose from not having the feedback it needs to have its products purchased through normal channels. Katy's company might lose because the bribing company might have a lower-quality product. Yes, there are a few "mights" here, which simply shows that the utilitarian principle isn't the strongest test available to Katy.

The **principle of justice** would produce more definite results for Katy. This test focuses on making sure that all decisions are based on fact and are consistent and unbiased. Fact here would be the quality of the product. Consistency would include the same bribe paid to all buyers in all companies the manufacturer deals with—an expensive idea. Bias—well, a bribe is unlikely to produce an unbiased decision. Thus, Katy would have to see the decision as unjust, based on this principle.

Notice that each of the four tests approaches the ethical issue from a different angle. If you use all four tests on any ethical decision you're faced with, you should be able to come up with a sound decision that violates neither your own conscience nor your position in the organization. In addition, use the following "ethics test."

This series of questions (see box) was invented at Bentley College in Boston and is often called the **Bentley College Ethics Test.**[1]

Bentley College Ethics Test

1. **Is this right?** This question assumes an absolute value of right or wrong—a universal guiding principle such as "thou shalt not kill" or "do unto others as you would have them do unto you" (the Golden Rule).

2. **Is this fair?** The Golden Rule puts forth a principle upon which a universal measure of fairness can be based. Would you feel you were being fairly treated if the tables were turned?

3. **Who, if anyone, gets hurt?** This question is based on the principle of utilitarianism. "Who stands to gain?" is the other side of this question. The next question is whether this is the person who *should* gain or lose (Who is deserving?).

4. **Would you be comfortable if the details of your decision were reported on the front page of your local newspaper?** If this question can only be answered no, ask yourself Why not? The answer should help you define the question.

5. **Would you tell your child (or young relative) to do this?** In other words, do you believe in this action strongly enough to teach it to an impressionable young person?

6. **How does this "smell"?** In other words, what does your intuition tell you about this course of action? To a sensible person, certain decisions simply "smell bad." If the answer to this question is "it stinks," explore your own mind to discover why.

This test is useful for going beyond the four tests above. They will help whenever you encounter a "gray area" in your life at work.

RATIONALIZATION

What if Katy uses both this test and the four principles we have mentioned and still decides to accept the money? She's probably rationalizing her action in some way. **Rationalization** is a way of in-

---

[1] "Ethics and the Bottom Line at Bentley," *Boston Globe*, Sept. 28, 1992, pp. 17, 19.

venting reasonable-sounding explanations for things that we often want to do for other, less defensible, reasons. Management expert Saul Gellerman warns that unethical behavior in the workplace often starts with one or more of **three basic rationalizations.**[2]

1. A belief that the chosen behavior is within ethical and legal limits—because it is comfortable and convenient to believe that it is. For example, a manager offers a day off with pay to an employee if the employee does not report an accident on the job.

2. A belief that "nobody will notice." Theft of a few cents from each depositor at a savings bank, for example, is likely to go unnoticed—or would it? Several cases are on record of just such a crime being discovered and prosecuted.

3. A belief that because the chosen action helps the company, the company will go along with it and protect the person if he or she is caught, or that the organization would *expect* that this action be carried out. For example, by paying a bribe and gaining a million-dollar customer, one salesperson thought that even if he was caught, the company would thank him for landing the account. Instead, he was fired.

Whenever you are expected to make a decision in a company, ask yourself, "Am I rationalizing, or am I approaching this decision honestly?" Notice that rationalizing unethical conduct is a form of lying to oneself—a bad habit to get into.

ARE SOME WORKPLACES UNETHICAL?

Have you ever worked for an organization that encouraged you to leave your ethics at the door when you come to work? Such workplaces do exist. Often, though, we exaggerate the extent to which management wants us to be unethical. Make sure that you are reading your managers fairly and that you are not assuming that you are expected to do things that most people in management wouldn't actually want you to do.[3]

---

[2] Saul W. Gellerman, "Why 'Good' Managers Make Bad Ethical Choices," *Harvard Business Review,* July–Aug., 1986, p. 88.

[3] Robert A. Cooke, "Danger Signs of Unethical Behavior: How to Determine if Your Firm Is at Ethical Risk," *Journal of Business Ethics,* 1991, pp. 249–53.

For example, Ramon was often asked to "fix" tickets at the truck stop where he ran the diesel pumps. Drivers would ask him to add $10 to the price of the fuel they bought, then split the difference with him—usually with the split unevenly going to the driver. Several of the drivers had told Ramon, "Your boss OKs this; it's the way things have always been done at this place." Later, his boss discovers what Ramon has been doing and fires him. Ramon should have asked his manager some questions early in his employment.

Everyone who works for a company or other organization should take a close look at their own personal ethics and then at the ethics of the workplace. How does your sense of personal ethics fit into the ethics of the larger group you work for and with? If you have to compromise to fit in, make sure the compromising doesn't force you to act against your own beliefs about what is right and wrong. Few situations cause more stress than compromising with our own consciences.

WHISTLE-BLOWING

When you discover unethical conduct in your own workplace, what should you do? One option you usually have is **whistle-blowing,** or turning in the offending person and exposing the truth to everybody. In our society, we have traditionally looked down upon the person who tells on someone else, especially in some areas of life. In grade school, for example, the tattletale is often looked down upon.

Many moral and ethical people are scared of blowing the whistle. After all, one's job might be at risk, or the whistle-blower might be shunned by others in the workplace. Others fear that people will misunderstand their intentions, that they will lose nerve at the last minute, or that deep down inside they are just jealous of the unethical person.

Here are some strategies that are open to you when you are in the position of a would-be whistle-blower:

1. Secretly threaten the offender with blowing the whistle unless the unethical action is stopped or corrected.
2. Secretly blow the whistle within the company, keeping your identity a secret.

3. Secretly threaten a responsible manager that you will blow the whistle outside of the company unless a change is made in the conduct.
4. Sabotage the results of the unethical behavior in some way.
5. Publicly blow the whistle within the organization.
6. Quietly refuse to carry out an unethical plan.
7. Secretly or publicly blow the whistle outside of the company.[4]

The reason some of the "sneakier" of these choices might be necessary is that many companies punish whistle-blowers in various ways for their honesty.[5] A new movement is afoot to encourage whistle-blowing in a few U.S. companies by providing rewards. Such a system, though, is likely to produce the negative effect of encouraging distrust among employees.

CHANGING ETHICS FROM THE TOP

The ethical tone of an organization nearly always originates in top management and moves downward. Thus, top management is in an ideal position to create an ethical environment for everyone who works in the company. One of the authors worked for a marketing company in Boston that was run by a group of managers who were always bragging about how they were "fooling the bigshots in California." (The company was a subsidiary of a larger firm in Los Angeles.) However, when these same managers discovered that many of the salespeople were faking their appointment schedules during training, they were surprised. They should have known that their unethical attitude would set the tone for employees.

Most of us will face ethical dilemmas in our lives. Knowing our own values and standards (see Chapter 5) is usually helpful, but some situations are still difficult to come to terms with. This chapter has not attempted to offer easy answers. There often are none. However, we hope you will have a greater awareness of the issues. To test your ethical awareness, take the test in the box that follows.

---

[4] Adapted from: Richard P. Nielsen, "Changing Unethical Organizational Behavior," *Executive*, May 1989, pp. 123–30.
[5] Sally Seymour, "The Case of the Willful Whistle-Blower," *Harvard Business Review*, Jan.–Feb. 1988, 103–9.

Testing Your Ethical Awareness

This ethics test will test your ethical awareness. Below are 20 statements that indicate decisions you might make under certain circumstances. Answer the questions as follows:

A for "always"   F for "frequently"   S for "sometimes"   N for "never"

You might have a job where some of these actions aren't possible. (For example, for question 5, your organization might not have a company car.) Answer such statements as if they were reading, "If I *were* in the position to . . . I would . . ."

1.	I use my organization's equipment for personal use.	A	F	S	N
2.	I take pens and pencils home for my own use.	A	F	S	N
3.	I spend more time on unscheduled breaks than I need to.	A	F	S	N
4.	I come to work late without my pay being affected.	A	F	S	N
5.	I use the company car for errands that aren't directly company related.	A	F	S	N
6.	I don't own up to mistakes I've made in my work.	A	F	S	N
7.	I blame others for mistakes I've made at work.	A	F	S	N
8.	I leave work early without taking a pay reduction.	A	F	S	N
9.	I call in sick to catch up on my sleep or recreation.	A	F	S	N
10.	I fill out paperwork for expenses that I didn't really incur.	A	F	S	N
11.	I take people I'm not doing business with out to lunch or dinner and charge the meal to the company.	A	F	S	N
12.	I use the company phone to make personal calls, including long-distance calls.	A	F	S	N
13.	I use the organization's copy machine for my personal use.	A	F	S	N
14.	I use company postage to mail personal letters.	A	F	S	N
15.	I tell company secrets to others.	A	F	S	N
16.	I will accept gifts from customers or suppliers in exchange for favors I give them.	A	F	S	N
17.	I have taken credit for an idea that wasn't really mine.	A	F	S	N
18.	I have given gifts or favors in exchange for preferential treatment.	A	F	S	N
19.	I purposely take longer to do some jobs than is necessary.	A	F	S	N
20.	I falsify reports to make myself look better.	A	F	S	N

KEY TO ETHICS TEST: Give yourself 1 point for each N answer, 2 points for each S answer, 3 points for each F answer, and 4 points for each A answer.

20–35, You're very ethical.

36–49, You could do some brushing up on ethics.

50–69, See a counselor.

70–80, You must be reading this book in prison.

Key Terms

ethics

morality

Golden Rule

categorical
  imperative

principle of
  utilitarianism

principle of justice

Bentley College
  Ethics Test

rationalization

three basic
  rationalizations

whistle-blowing

Review Questions

1. Briefly define *ethics* as the term applies to your own values.
2. Which of the ethics tests included in this chapter appeals to you as the soundest and most useful? Why?
3. Briefly explain the "three basic rationalizations" for unethical behavior. Which, if any, have you been tempted to use to justify questionable actions? Be honest.
4. Briefly explain the six parts of the Bentley College Ethics Test. How can you apply this test in your own workplace?
5. What is your own position on whistle-blowing? Would you blow the whistle on misconduct in your own company? How unethical would the conduct have to be before you would do so?

Multiple Choice

1. Which of the following is the best definition of *ethics?*
   a. Morality and consequences of actions.
   b. Standards of conduct and morals in a particular society, which are based on the past and respected in the present.
   c. The methods of going about getting what we want from and for other members of our society.
   d. Behavior in our society that may or may not be rationalized.
2. Ethical issues are:
   a. The same as legal issues.
   b. Usually a problem only in small companies.
   c. Usually a problem only in large corporations.
   d. Relevant to everyone in business.
3. When we make plausible-sounding excuses for unethical behavior, we are:

    a. Postponing.

    b. Rationalizing.

    c. Categorizing.

    d. Pardoning

4. Which of these is *not* a question from the Bentley College Ethics Test?

    a. Ask, Is this right?

    b. Ask, Is this expensive?

    c. Ask, How does this "smell"?

    d. Ask, Would you be comfortable if your decision were reported on the front page of the newspaper?

5. When you turn someone in for unethical conduct, you are known as a:

    a. Rubbernecker.

    b. Jostler.

    c. Whistle-blower.

    d. Troublemaker.

Case
10–1

The Rotating Expense Report

Ed Roseman is the accounts supervisor for Elgin Software. He and Dave McKown have recently become friends. McKown is the shop manager for manufacturing and thus has the largest payroll and expense accounts at Elgin.

Accounts for each month are settled by the fourth of the following month, including travel expenses, minor office items, and so forth. On April 3, Dave came into Ed's office. "Ed, I wonder if you'll do me a favor. I have about $100 worth of items I need you to include on your own expense voucher. Last month, mine was really overloaded. And because management has been making such a big deal about personal expense items, I was hoping you could put the $100 on your own account. You were just mentioning last week that yours has been light this month. It really isn't any big deal; you can just give me the hundred in cash when you get it. In fact, why don't you keep 10 bucks for your trouble; just give me 90 and we'll be even. What do you say?" Ed said he'd give it some thought.

Back at his desk, Ed thinks long and hard about Dave's request. Finally, he decides that he's going to have to say no. Once before in his professional life, Ed had let friendship compromise his sense of ethical conduct. He hadn't gotten caught, but the incident had been eating at him for six years. I don't need something else to feel guilty about, Ed says to himself as he sends an E-mail to Dave. The message begins, "Dave, we need to talk in person . . ."

1. If you were Ed at this point, what exactly would you say to Dave? Why?

2. In terms of your own view of ethics, how unethical was the action Ed was being asked to take?

3. How do you think this episode will affect the friendship between these two men?

PART TWO

II

Fitting into the Group—Should You?

LaQuita and Tasha were sitting in the computer lab of their business college, talking about a new student, Kendra.

LaQuita: Can you believe her? I would never do what she does—sit on the desk during class. No way! And just get up and walk out during class. That is so *rude!*

Tasha: [*whispering*] And have you noticed that when she comes in late, she walks in through the front door—right in front of the instructor while she's talking? I've never seen anyone else do that! And yesterday after class she pulled on the instructor's arm to get her attention!

LaQuita: Well, she just doesn't get it. She doesn't know how to act here. She's not going to make any friends, and I bet the placement center has a hard time getting her a job after she graduates, too! She won't know how to act in an interview!

In the story above, Kendra is acting in a way that will probably not allow her to become part of her school group. We all need to belong to a group. In the words of the ancient Greek philosopher Aristotle, we are all "social animals." When we are infants we need to be a part of a group to survive, and we have a strong need to be part of a group throughout our lives.

What is a group? How are groups formed? Why do we belong to them? Is conformity to groups good or bad? These are some of the questions we will answer in this chapter.

WHAT ARE GROUPS?

A group can be defined as two or more people who are together for any purpose. People in a group may interact with only one other person; for example, by sending each other electronic mail; or they may interact in a large group; for example, when hundreds of people are attending a national conference. Group members share goals. Sometimes these goals are as simple as keeping friendships going, and sometimes they are as complex as taking part in successful union negotiations.

People in a group behave by the group's rules. These may be unspoken and simple rules, such as not starting the book club meeting until all members have gotten a cup of coffee. But they also may be formal rules, such as voting on all actions taken at every meeting. Group members maintain stable role relationships; for example, the president of the club always runs the meeting. Groups also form subgroups when a few members come together and others break apart. These subgroups may form because a subcommittee needs to work on a project, or the subgroups may be people who become friends and then later the friendship fades.

THE PURPOSES OF GROUPS

We join groups to fill the needs that we can't fulfill alone. These needs fit into the following several categories.[1]

1. Affiliation.   We all have a basic need to be with other people, and to relate to others. Some of us have a stronger need to affiliate than others, but we all need to belong.

2. Proximity.   We often form groups just because we need to form

---

[1] Robert N. Lussier, *Supervision: A Skill-Building Approach* (Homewood IL: Richard D. Irwin, 1989), p. 418.

ties with people whom we see frequently. These include people we work with, go to school with, live near, and so on.

3. **Attraction.**   We are usually attracted to people who are like us and people whom we like, or people who are the way we would like to become. We are drawn to people who have attitudes, values, personalities, and economic positions similar to ours. We also like to be around people we find attractive.

4. **Activities.**   We often join groups that are involved in activities that interest us. These can be structured groups, such as a service organization; or unstructured, such as friends who go rock-climbing together.

5. **Assistance.**   Sometimes we join groups because of the help the group can give us in some area of our lives. La Leche League is an example of an assistance group, formed to help nursing mothers who have questions about breastfeeding infants.

SOCIALIZATION

We all need to learn what rules our society has set for people to follow. When we learn and follow these rules, we will be successful within our own social groups or society. This process of learning our society's rules is called **socialization.** We are socialized by many people throughout our lives: our parents, schoolteachers, friends, spouses, children and grandchildren, political and religious leaders, and the mass media. The process of socialization can be very obvious, such as when our parents tell us to share our toys with our friends. It can also be less obvious, such as when our hairstyle is not quite right, and our friends let us know by their odd looks or giggling.

SOCIAL NORMS

The unwritten rules each society has set for its members are called **social norms.** Different societies have different social norms. For example, all societies have different rules about **proximity,** or how far apart we should stand from each other. In our society, we stand about two to three feet apart in normal conversations, and about a foot apart when talking to intimate friends, lovers, or spouses. But in other cultures, for example, in the Middle East, normal proximity is much closer.

Social norms have a very powerful influence on how we behave. To see for yourself just how powerful they are, try standing too close to someone, for example, a roommate or a store clerk. Does that person seem to feel uncomfortable? Do you? Or try facing the wrong way in an elevator. Just the fact that you know which is the "wrong" way (facing the sides or back of the elevator) tells you how influential social norms are. Look at the reactions of people around you when you do so. Are they uncomfortable? Are you?

FORMAL GROUPS

We have all belonged to different groups since we were children. Some of the groups have a formal structure and are called **formal groups**. These include groups such as the school chorus, student government, or a company's planning committee. Becoming a member of a formal group isn't always up to us; sometimes we are voted in or selected to it.

INFORMAL GROUPS

While formal groups have structure, other groups called **informal groups** just seem to happen. Informal groups include people with special interests and hobbies, particular habits, or personality traits. Leaders in informal groups either appoint themselves as leaders, because no one else steps up, or they are appointed by group agreement. Since there is no formal structure involved, informal groups are always changing. These kinds of groups are found everywhere—at work or in personal settings.

STATUS IN GROUPS

In any group, the respect that group members have for each other is not equal. Individuals in groups hold different ranks, depending on the group's values. **Status** is the rank that people hold within a group. Status can be based on many different sources, either formal or informal. For example, in a job situation, status in a group is based on a person's formal position within the company—vice-president of business affairs, for example. Other informal factors that can be sources of rank or status are interpersonal or social skills, personal charm or charisma, educational level, physical appearance, intelligence, persuasive ability, or athletic ability. We can all think back to high school when status within groups depended on some of these factors; intelligence and athletic ability are common sources of status in that setting.

Group members with high status usually have a lot of influence on group decisions and group morale. A factor related to a person's status within a group is **status acceptance.** If you have lower status in a group than you feel you deserve, your own morale and the group's morale will be affected in a negative way. The opposite situation is true, also; giving someone more status than the member feels that he or she deserves can cause problems, too. People with high self-esteem usually attain higher status than those with low self-esteem, and they are usually more content with the status level that the group has given them.

CONFORMITY IN GROUPS

After group norms have been set and status issues have been worked out, **conformity** can be an issue. *Conformity* means acting the same way as the group and agreeing with group decisions. One reason why members of groups conform is to avoid being rejected by the group. Think back to high school again. Within each social group, members probably dressed alike, talked alike, listened to the same music, hung out at the same place after school, and held the same beliefs. We were usually able to identify the groups that students belonged to based on their appearance. At this time in a person's life—adolescence—conformity is high because acceptance is very important. But as adults, why do we conform? Is conformity good or bad?

Groups need a certain amount of conformity if they are going to be able to function. It would be hard to keep a group together if no one could agree or conform! But there is an ugly side to conformity, too. Too much conformity can make people afraid to say what is on their minds. This will kill creativity and new ideas.

GROUPTHINK

There are several famous examples of situations where high group conformity led to very serious or dangerous outcomes. President Kennedy and his advisers almost brought the United States to war over the Bay of Pigs incident; President Nixon's staff became involved in the Watergate scandal due to high conformity; and the fatal explosion of the space shuttle *Challenger* can be blamed in part on high conformity among the group of people who knew about a potential danger to the shuttle. This type of dangerous high conformity is called **groupthink.**[2]

Groups are especially vulnerable to the dangers of groupthink when all think along the same lines, hold the same beliefs and goals, close themselves off to outside information, are under pressure, believe they have the best solution to a problem, and believe that what they are doing is right. In groups that have problems with groupthink, there is often a **mindguard** in the group who keeps disagreement out of the group. A mindguard is a self-appointed member of the group who sees his or her job as protecting the group form information that would call the group's decision into question. Just as a bodyguard protects someone from physical harm, a mindguard protects the group from disagreeable facts. See the box for ways to overcome groupthink.

Overcoming Groupthink

1. Expect all members of a group to participate in the decision-making process.
2. Set up smaller sub-groups that are assigned to come up with the solutions to the same projects.
3. Invite outside experts into the group.
4. Appoint a **"devil's advocate"** within the group to consider other options.
5. Set up a timeline to consider the competitor's position.

---

[2] Irving Janis, *Groupthink,* 2nd ed. (New York: Houghton Mifflin, 1982).

Although we need to belong to groups, too much conformity is not a good thing. Keeping our own identity and sticking with our own opinions while being in a group makes the group work better.

 # Key Terms

socialization	informal groups	groupthink
social norms	status	mindguard
proximity	status acceptance	"devil's advocate"
formal groups	conformity	

 # Review Questions

1. What are the dangers of groupthink? Have you experienced groupthink in situations in your own life? If so, what were the outcomes?
2. In addition to the social norms on proximity, what other social norms can you see happening in the group (school, work, family) around you right now? Try violating a simple social norm. What happens?
3. Do you agree with Aristotle's quote that we are all "social animals"? Can you think of any situations where we could survive without others?
4. We are all socialized, all of the time. In what situations do *you* socialize others?
5. What formal and informal groups do you belong to? Do these groups follow their own sets of group rules? What are these rules?

Multiple Choice

1. One of the ways to reduce the negative effects of groupthink is to:
   a. Appoint a mindguard.
   b. Appoint a "devil's advocate."
   c. Close off the group to outsiders.
   d. Increase the pressure on the group to come to a decision.

2. Socialization can be defined as:
   a. Spending free time with our friends.
   b. Learning the rules of a culture or group.
   c. Learning what good manners are in public.
   d. Having fun in a group.
3. Ashley has just joined a ski club. Her main motivation for joining this group is probably:
   a. Affiliation
   b. Activities
   c. Assistance
   d. Attraction
4. Elizabeth gets together between classes at college for a cup of coffee with friends every Wednesday and Friday. This is an example of:
   a. A formal group
   b. An informal group
   c. A conformity group
   d. A mindguard group
5. Wendy feels that she should have been elected president of the Entrepreneurs Club, but she didn't get nominated for any club office. The negative feelings she has now are probably a result of problems with:
   a. Status acceptance
   b. Groupthink
   c. Conformity
   d. Socialization

Case
11–1

Mexi-Cali Restaurant

Alyssa and Kirby were keeping busy trying to look busy washing dishes at the restaurant where they were working.

Alyssa: Quick, Kirby, here comes "Nasty Natalie," the meanest boss on earth. Hand me that salsa bowl!

Kirby: Here's the bowl. Hey, Alyssa, why does everybody in the kitchen staff call her that, anyway? She's always been nice to me. She changes my schedule when I need her to, and she even gave me a ride home one time!

Alyssa: I don't know who made up the name. But if you want the rest of us here to cover for you and make your job a whole lot easier, you'd better learn to go along with the program at Mexi-Cali Restaurant!

Kirby: Now that you mention it, I guess "Nasty Natalie" does give me mean looks sometime. I guess she's not that cool.

Alyssa: You know, Kirby, I think you'll fit in just fine here. Now let's get these dishes washed up and get out of here.

1. Who is conforming in this situation, and why? Is this type of conformity good or bad for the people involved?

2. What are some of the social norms for this restaurant staff?

3. Is the larger group in this situation a formal group or an informal group? Why?

12

Improving Climate: The Indoor Weather of the Workplace

Nadine was hired as an office receptionist in a doctor's office. As she approached her new job, she was confident that her many years of experience in medical work would stand her in good stead. Before long, though, it became clear that this was no ordinary physician's practice. The doctor seemed constantly unhappy with everyone on the staff, for reasons Nadine couldn't understand. He also made patients wait for long periods of time while he read magazines and made personal phone calls. The climate was always tense; rarely did anyone laugh or act relaxed. Although the pay was good, Nadine was searching for another job by the end of the first week.

Nadine had encountered a negative organizational climate—a workplace "weather" that was constantly cloudy and bleak. Although finding another position is certainly an option for someone in her place, both workers and managers can take some other actions to improve their workplace climate.

WHAT IS ORGANIZATIONAL CLIMATE?

Organizational climate is often defined as the way the workplace feels to the people who work there. One reason that climate is important is because the way workers perceive the workplace also affects their *attitudes* toward the environment where they spend most of their time.

Organizational climate has many components, including:

- **Certainty versus uncertainty.** The amount of certainty and the amount of risk taking allowed are climate factors in the workplace.
- **Personal warmth.** The degree to which workers relate to each other with feelings is an important climate factor.
- **Control.** The amount of control that workers are allowed compared with how much they are controlled by managers or schedules figures into overall workplace climate.
- **Supportiveness.** The amount of support and encouragement given to workers by management and by each other is a climate factor
- **Punishments versus rewards.** How are workers disciplined for breaking rules? To what extent are they rewarded for a job well done?
- **Physical appearance of the workplace.** This category includes color schemes, dress codes, placement of desks and equipment, and so forth.
- **Company pride and loyalty.** To what extent are workers proud to be a part of the organization? Will they be loyal to it and to other workers?

DIFFERENT TYPES OF CLIMATE

Before you try to change your workplace climate, take a close look at the type of climate you have—in terms of all of the issues we just discussed. Different climates stress different aspects of the workplace.

The "Productivity Climate"

In the "productivity climate," the entire emphasis of the organization is on productivity. "Getting the job done at all costs" often outweighs more human and humane considerations. The managers who create this type of environment are usually seen as distant, cold, and difficult to talk to. Some types of businesses almost require the productivity climate. To be fair to managers, they are not

always the cause of this climate type. If your workplace is like this
try the following:

1. **Humanize.** Whether you are a manager or a worker, do
   your part to insert the human element whenever possible.
   Create an awareness that the people in this workplace are
   human beings with human feelings and needs.
2. **Communicate.** The productivity climate breaks down
   most often in the area of interpersonal communication, including writing, talking, and listening. Encourage others
   to improve in all three areas.
3. **Be productive.** Don't work against productive spirit. The
   climate requires it, so don't run against the flow, at least in
   this respect.

The "Laissez-Faire" Climate

Laissez-faire is a French term that means "allow to act." In the
laissez-faire climate, workers are given tremendous freedom to act
as they desire. This climate is thus permissive, allowing for great individual initiative and freedom, but with all of the pitfalls such an
approach probably suggests to you—lack of control, lack of accountability, and lack of direction. Yet, in some organizations, a laissez-faire approach works. A good example: A medical clinic manager certainly doesn't need to provide scheduling, discipline, or
structure for the physicians who work there.

   If you find yourself in an organization with this climate, ask
yourself first if this climate "works" in your organization. If the answer is no, try the following.

If you are a manager:

1. **Create a structure.** Provide a structure for workers to perform in. How strict and tight that structure needs to be
   will depend on the nature of both work and workers.
2. **Provide an evaluation system.** No control system will
   work without a method of evaluating its success or failure.

If you are an employee:

1. **Manage yourself.** Learn to be your own best boss. Nobody else is likely to create a structure for you. Create it for

yourself. Be sure your task is completed satisfactorily and be concerned with the tasks of others only if they affect you directly.

2. **Motivate yourself.** Create a self-rewarding motivation system that works for you. For example, you could set a quota of work for yourself. When the goal is reached, give yourself a 20-minute break.

The Participative Climate

Of all climate types, the **participative climate** is the most difficult to achieve. Getting everyone to participate in decision making is a goal that an organization often speaks of but doesn't quite achieve. A participative climate is one in which people want to be involved in the decisions that affect them daily. Workers are motivated and involved, and managers coach and coordinate rather than rule with an iron hand. A supervisor functions much the same as the captain of an athletic team: a leader and a team member at the same time. A supervisor works to create a team spirit in which individuals work in harmony for the goals of the team instead of seeking glory for themselves.

Research has shown that the participative climate, when working as it should, creates the best worker attitudes and the least worker turnover. If it's so good, why don't more workplaces use it? One reason is that the old authority-figure management has such a long tradition in our society that it is very difficult to train managers and supervisors to become team leaders. Another is that not all workers deal well with this type of climate; some actually prefer to be told what to do. Still another reason is that individual egos must be subdued for the team approach to succeed. Some people simply find that a participative environment cannot take care of their ego needs.

STEPS TO A BETTER ORGANIZATIONAL CLIMATE

Whatever type of climate you find yourself in—one of the three above or a combination of two or all of them—there are steps you can take to improve the climate where you work. An effective climate allows people to work to their full potential without becoming a threat to each other. It encourages workers to complete tasks on time and well.

Changing the Climate

Admittedly, sweeping climate changes are best done by managers and must have their support to succeed. Before beginning, a manager should look carefully at the organizational climate as it now is. Which factors most hinder productivity and morale? Why? Ask the workers what changes they would suggest. One effective format is a question such as, "If a new worker were to begin here today, what characteristics of this place would you warn him or her about?" A candid answer to that question from every employee can be very helpful in assessing the current organizational climate.

Changing an organization's climate is not like changing its culture. Unlike corporate culture, a workplace climate often can be changed quite rapidly, though not always easily. If you're a supervisor, your own attitude is the most important single factor in such change. Show the employees that you really want the change to happen and that the changes will be good both for the organization and for them individually. If you are an employee, any climate change might be individual, in your own corner of the workplace. You might be surprised how much your positive attitude can do to at least improve the climate of that corner of your reality.

1. Develop a shared vision of the new climate you want in the workplace. Be sure that everyone knows the changes are going to happen and when.

2. Involve everyone. Anybody whose work life is to be affected in any way by the climate change should be actively involved in that change. Get employees started as early as possible in the process, even in the decision to make the change, if that is feasible.

3. Make cosmetic and symbolic changes. Don't be afraid that someone will see a new color of paint in an office or a new phone system as superficial. Such changes, especially when timed to be put in place at the same time as more substantive changes, can be meaningful in establishing the new atmosphere that you want.

4. Change job assignments when necessary. If you find job duties redundant, unequal, unfairly distributed, or confusing, change job descriptions to reflect the new climate. Most importantly, use human resources effectively, wasting as little talent as possible.

5. Don't forget motivation. One of the main reasons for improving workplace climate is to motivate workers. Whatever changes you come up with, ask yourself, What is the most likely to motivate the workers and myself on a long-term basis? (See Chapter 6).

Organizational climate is a most important factor. Like the weather outside, it affects our ability to cope and to be productive. The old saying, "Everyone complains about the weather, but nobody does anything about it," is all too often true of indoor climate as well. Be a manager or employee who is different. Be one who does something about it.

 ## Key Terms

organizational climate	punishments versus rewards	"productivity climate"
certainty versus uncertainty	physical appearance of workplace	laissez-faire climate
personal warmth		participative climate
control	company pride and loyalty	
supportiveness		cosmetic and symbolic changes

 ## Review Questions

1. What is meant by organizational climate? Why is it called the indoor weather of the workplace?
2. What are the components of any organizational climate? List and explain each.
3. Of the three climate types—productivity climate, laissez-faire climate, or participative climate—which one would you prefer to be a part of? Why?
4. Briefly explain the steps to take in changing the climate of an

organization. If you are not a manager, can you ever be involved in such change?

5. In your opinion, what characteristics would constitute a perfect organizational climate? Create an ideal version of reality that would contain all of these qualities.

Multiple Choice

1. Which of the following is the *best* definition of organizational climate?
   a. The way the "feeling" of the workplace is seen by those who work there.
   b. A system of shared values.
   c. The standards and ethics of the organization.
   d. The extent to which democracy is practiced in the workplace.

2. Which of the following statements about organizational climate is *true*?
   a. Organizational climate cannot be changed.
   b. Organizational climate affects the motivation of workers.
   c. The productivity climate is the best one in all ways.
   d. Organizational climate is always negative, never positive.

3. Which of the following is *not* one of the ways to improve the productivity climate?
   a. Humanize
   b. Communicate
   c. Advertise
   d. Be productive.

4. Of all the climate types, which one is the *most difficult* to achieve?
   a. Productivity climate
   b. Socialistic climate
   c. Laissez-faire climate
   d. Participative climate

5. If your manager repaints your office and installs a new phone system, he or she is probably:
   a. Wasting time and money.
   b. Making cosmetic and symbolic changes.
   c. Attempting both climate and culture change at the same time.
   d. Attempting to get rid of you.

Case 12–1

The New Office

When Joan Harrington was given a chance to join the marketing department of a successful urban corporation, she was thrilled. She didn't think twice about quitting her job as advertising manager of a small rural television station. This was the big time, and working with other experienced advertising people looked like a perfect learning experience.

Before long, though, Joan noticed that this new workplace was considerably different from her former TV station. Everyone seemed to be cynical about management, about the company itself, and about work. The idea of working overtime without pay, as she had sometimes done at her old job, was considered unthinkable.

At the end of the first week, Joan found herself wondering if this was where she really belonged. By the end of the second week, she was finding it increasingly difficult just to get out of the house and off to work each morning. "What have I done to myself?" she muttered to herself as she entered the company on the second Friday morning.

1. Are there any steps Joan can take to improve her lot? Can she do anything to help create a better climate for work? If so, what?

2. What would you do if you were in Joan's position? Why?

3. How could some knowledge about the workplace climate help Joan in her new environment?

13

Hey! Are You Listening?

Sometimes when we talk, we just need to be heard. All of us have a very strong need to have other people hear us, understand us, and process the information we give them. This need is so strong that when listening is withheld, our self-esteem often suffers.

This tremendous need to be listened to is crucial to human relations. We should realize that other people have this need as much as we do. You'll be amazed at the results you can get once you become tuned into other people and their needs. The need to be a good listener is often ignored by people who consider themselves good communicators. In fact, nearly everyone is a poor listener. Right after most of us hear someone else talk, we remember only half of what we have heard—no matter how carefully we thought we were listening. Two months after listening to a talk, the average listener will remember only about 25 percent of what was said.[1] Thus, although we need badly to be heard, we don't return the favor. How good a listener are you? Take the listening test in the box on the next page.

SELECTIVE LISTENING

Let's start with some of the more legitimate reasons for poor listening. In our society we are bombarded with messages. Because we

---

[1] Frank K. Sonnenberg, "Barriers to Communication," *The Journal of Business Strategy* (Volume 11, July/August 1990), 56–58.

Listening Test

	Always	Often	Sometimes	Never
1. The people I talk to feel that I understand what they are trying to say.	—	—	—	—
2. I pretend to be listening more than I really am.	—	—	—	—
3. The way people talk distracts me from listening to what they are really saying.	—	—	—	—
4. I ask people to repeat what they have said.	—	—	—	—
5. I notice nonverbal signals while I am listening to others.	—	—	—	—
6. I maintain eye contact while I am in a conversation with someone else.	—	—	—	—
7. I finish other people's sentences.	—	—	—	—
8. I can usually tell by looking at someone whether that person will be worth listening to.	—	—	—	—
9. I make a real effort to understand the other person's point of view.	—	—	—	—
10. I end conversations that aren't interesting to me by changing the subject.	—	—	—	—
11. I nod, smile, frown, or use some other facial expression to let the speaker know I am listening.	—	—	—	—
12. I am usually putting together my response while the other person is still speaking.	—	—	—	—
13. I act on the belief that many people aren't worth listening to.	—	—	—	—
14. My mind wanders when I'm in a group listening to a speaker.	—	—	—	—
15. I try to put myself in the speaker's place.	—	—	—	—

(See page 118 for scoring results.)

couldn't possibly give our full attention to all of these messages, we become **selective listeners.** If we are in a personal environment with even more demands on our attention, the problem is even greater. For example, picture a home with younger children chattering and trying to get attention. Parents often become selective listeners if only to retain their sanity. Busy workplaces can affect us the same way. Thus, **information overload** is one cause of poor listening skills.

Many other reasons for bad listening, though, come from habits we have established through our lives. For example, when a subject seems difficult—above our level of ability—we will often fail to listen. If we had listened, we would have seen how clear and understandable the subject was. The opposite often happens as well. We might reject a speaker because the message seems too basic, beneath our level of knowledge. In either case, the message is lost.

When we are in a group listening to a single speaker, we easily allow our minds to wander because we have a capacity for listening at a speed that far exceeds the ability of the fastest speaker to speak. We *could* listen and comprehend up to 500 words per minute. The average public speaker, however, delivers a speech at about 125 words per minute. How we spend that extra time and energy often determines our effectiveness as listeners.[2] If we are attending a business meeting or conference, the potential benefits of attending the meeting can be destroyed by such habits of bad listening.

TUNING OUT

Sometimes, we simply refuse to listen to our co-workers. This is called **tuning out.** Often it results from prejudice. Some people won't listen to members of races they consider inferior; some men won't listen to women. Prejudice can be more subtle than these blatant examples, though. What about a person who looks unintelligent to the listener or whose appearance is in some other way unattractive? Prejudice can also overlap with jealousy. What about a speaker who seems just a little bit too perfect? We need to watch

---

[2] Ibid., p. 56.

our listening habits to rule out these types of prejudice. The process of doing business can be hampered by prejudice. We will approach the topic of prejudice more fully in Chapter 27.

"Red flag" words and expressions can bring an immediate emotional response from the listener. All of us have words that send our minds off in another emotional direction when we hear them. Often a word will trigger a reaction because of strong beliefs we have on a subject. In many cases, the reaction is negative. A word such as "communist," for example, might begin a flood of emotions that would keep some people from hearing anything else for quite a while. A word such as "sex" might get similar results, although the emotions from the word would likely be more positive.[3]

Clearly, there are many reasons why we do not hear what our co-workers are really saying. Listening expert Anthony Allesandra says that one major reason underlies most of our poor listening habits. From childhood on, we have been taught that *talking* requires energy, attention, and organization, but that listening is a passive, compliant position. From kindergarten onward, we are taught to be assertive, to express ourselves effectively. Until recently, though, little has been done to teach us "active listening," as Allesandra calls it.[4]

HOW TO BECOME A BETTER LISTENER

What can we do to become active listeners? We can all change our listening habits, but as with all habits, these changes take time and effort.

1. **Stop talking.**   If you are talking, time and opportunity to talk are being taken away from the other person or persons. This is the first and, in many ways, the most important rule.

2. **Get rid of distractions.**   Distractions can be external, such as noise and movements near you, or internal thoughts and emotions.

---

[3] Lyle Sussman and Paul D. Krivonos, *Communication for Supervisors and Managers* (Alfred Publishing, 1979), pp. 66–68.

[4] Anthony Allesandra, quoted in *The Power of Listening* (CRM Films, 1987).

Moving closer to the speaker, changing your physical position, putting those nagging personal problems out of your mind are all ways of **eliminating distractions.**

3. Use pauses for reflecting. When a speaker pauses, use the extra time to make associations in your mind with other things that have been said. Think of your past experiences so that you can see relationships among the ideas being offered. Avoid the temptation to let your mind wander.

4. Listen for main ideas. When listening to a public speaker, jot down key words and phrases. Take note of repeated ideas. Try as early as possible to see the outline headings the speaker is using. When talking one-on-one, make sure you understand each point made by the speaker.

5. Give feedback. Many people mistakenly think of **feedback** only as communication in a one-on-one situation. Eye contact and facial expressions, though, are examples of feedback that can be given in nearly any situation. When talking with one other person, you should respond with an **"I" statement.** Instead of saying, "Your ideas on this project are hard to understand," the speaker should say something like, "I feel that an important step has been left out. Why don't you examine the marketing plan before you proceed?"

6. Listen for feelings as well as facts. Most people can understand the facts a speaker is presenting. Tuning in on the emotions behind those facts requires careful listening. Some of that listening can be done with your eyes. Watch for nonverbal messages that will help you understand how the speaker *feels* about the subject. Eye and body movements, vocal tone, and posture are examples. We will deal more with nonverbal communication later in this chapter. By listening for feelings, you also will become more aware of your own feelings about what you're hearing.

7. Paraphrase. **Paraphrasing** means saying the same thing you just heard, but in your own words. This technique is effective because it not only allows for clearer understanding, it also lets the other speaker know that you have cared enough to take what was said and process it into your own language. Paraphrased responses can start with a question such as, "Do you mean . . . ?" or "What I hear you saying is . . ." Try this step when you are in a hostile situation—when the other person has an intense need to be understood. You are likely to be surprised at the positive results.

8. **Encourage others to talk.** Encouraging others to talk can make you more responsible for what you say yourself. An added bonus is that you will be less likely to jump to conclusions about the speaker's intent. In a public speaking situation, this means allowing others to be involved when the speaker calls for questions.

Notice how many of these eight steps have to do with self-esteem. If you feel good about yourself, using all eight of these strategies will be both easier and more effective. Although it might sound too simple, people who like themselves tend to be better listeners.

Becoming an Empathic Listener

Empathic listening means putting oneself into the other person's shoes, so to speak, and entering the other person's world. To be a truly empathic listener, you must temporarily make the other person's reality more important than your own. Doing that is not easy, especially if you are not in the habit of thinking in such a way. Remember that to the other person, his or her reality is extremely important—more important than yours, unless the other person is either exceptionally unselfish or has learned this skill already.

Before even beginning to listen, prepare yourself to enter the world of the speaker. The starting point is understanding that the other person has very real needs. If it's a public speaker, listen and watch for signals you can use as clues about where the speaker is "coming from."

Key Terms

selective listeners	active listening	paraphrasing
information overload	eliminating distractions	encouraging others to talk
tuning out	feedback	empathic listening
"red flag" words	"I" statement	

Review Questions

1. Think of people you have been around who are poor listeners. Do they all have certain qualities in common? If so, what are they?

2. Are you ever the victim of information overload? Why? What steps can you take to ensure that you can avoid information overload in the future?
3. List the eight steps toward better listening and explain each with an example.
4. Define and explain the use of "I" statements in the communication process.
5. Are you usually an empathic listener? If not, do you know anyone who is? What qualities set an empathic listener apart from other people?

Multiple Choice

1. When many different demands are being made on us for our attention, we often slip into what is known as:
   a. Lack of caring
   b. Selective listening
   c. Overload listening
   d. Empathic listening
2. Step 1 in "How to Become a Better Listener" is:
   a. Concentrate on what the speaker is saying.
   b. Concentrate on what you are going to say in return to the speaker.
   c. Stop talking.
   d. Listen for facts rather than feelings.
3. Words and expression that bring an immediate emotional response from the listener are known as:
   a. Frustration derivative words
   b. Third-dimension words
   c. Information overload words
   d. Red flag words
4. Which of the following is *not* one of the reasons why people fail to listen?
   a. Other people talk too fast.
   b. Information overload.
   c. Assumptions one often makes about the subject.
   d. We see listening as a passive, compliant activity.
5. When we are trying to heed too many messages at once, we fall victims of:
   a. Threshold fever

b. Information overload
c. Pretentious listening
d. Feigned listening

Scoring Key for Listening Test

Score questions 1,5,6,9,11, and 15 as follows: 4 points for each "always," 3 points for each "often," 2 points each for each "sometimes," and 0 points for each "never." For questions 2,3,4,7,8,10,12,13, and 14, score 4 points for each "never," 3 points for each "sometimes," 2 points for each "often," and 0 points for each "always."

52–60	You're an excellent listener.
45–51	Although you're not a nonlistener, you're not as much fun to talk with as you could be.
38–44	Your listening habits need some serious attention.
30–37	People probably avoid spending much time talking with you.
0–29	Read this chapter over again; you need it!

Case 13–1

The Birthday Party

Jason Strong and Walt Wheeler both work in customer service at a large auto parts distributor. Their manager has often told them that they have the freedom to cover workstations of the other 18 customer service people as long as all stations are covered at all times. Jason's daughter's birthday is coming up and his wife has been urging him to attend.

In the lunchroom, Jason is taking his break when Walt walks in.

Jason: Hey, Walt, I have to be off next Tuesday afternoon for about four hours. I was noticing that you aren't on then. Could you cover for me so I can go see Liz turn six?

Walt: No problem.

Jason: Great. I owe you one.

The conversation quickly turned to other issues, and the favor wasn't mentioned again.

On Tuesday afternoon, customer service was especially hard hit with trouble calls. "Where's Jason Strong?" Deborah James, the manager, wanted to know. When she saw Walt's name entered in Jason's place for the afternoon, James called Walt at home, only to hear his voice mail. Two hours later, Walt Wheeler ran into the department, apologizing profusely.

1. How was listening an issue in this case?
2. What could Jason Strong have done to prevent this problem from happening? How about Walt Wheeler?
3. If you were the manager, what steps could you take to prevent this type of problem from occurring in the future?

14

About Those Nonverbals!

"Do you believe the boss when he says there won't be any cuts in the staff?" one worker asks the other after a staff meeting. "No, and I'll tell you why," the other replies. "It's because his voice says one thing, but his behavior says something else. What I hear him really saying is something like 'Gee, I hope the cuts in staff won't come, but I'm not really sure.'"

The boss's body language was giving him away. Body language is only one type of a larger set of expressions that we call nonverbal behavior. Our nonverbal behavior is a powerful communicator. It usually tells the truth, whether or not our words do so. Even when we are not in touch with our own true feelings on an issue, our nonverbal behavior will often give us away, apparently because our unconscious mind controls our nonverbal signals. But communicating honesty to others isn't the only function of nonverbal behavior. We need to understand the nonverbal signals others are sending to us, but it is just as important to become more aware of the way we are coming across to others.

WHAT NONVERBAL MESSAGES DO

Experts tell us that there are three major uses of nonverbal messages in our communicating. They show the *feelings and emotions* of the speaker. They help *clarify* what is being said in words. They show the *emotional reactions* of the speaker to other people whether those reactions are negative, positive, or mixed.[1] Let's look at each of these functions in more detail.

1. Showing the speaker's feelings and emotions.   Our words don't always express our real feelings. Sometimes that fact is a matter of choice. Often, though, we unknowingly give away the feelings that we haven't even put into words. **Showing emotion** can take the form of fear, uncertainty, inferiority, and discomfort, to name a few. If someone's nonverbal messages disagree with the spoken words, which one should you believe? The answer is nearly always the nonverbals—the body language.

What is the lesson for the person who is trying to improve human relations skills? Beware of your feelings and emotions because, unless you are a practiced actor, they will show themselves when you communicate with others. When we communicate unconsciously, our internal climate—how we feel within ourselves— is bound to give us away. If we are feeling bad about ourselves, that will show. Of course, if we are feeling *good* about ourselves, that will show, too. If we have other issues on our mind, our lack of complete attention is likely to get in the way of real communication. Self-esteem is the key to internal climate.

Let's say you are a retail clerk. A customer comes up to you, acting very nervous and tense. Her eyes dart back and forth and she does not keep steady eye contact with you. No matter what this customer finally says, you are likely to be especially tuned in to the body language. Maybe she has just observed a shoplifter; maybe she *is* the shoplifter! Your own nonverbal reactions to such a speaker will be very important to what happens next.

2. Clarifying messages.   Have you ever talked for a long time on the telephone to someone you have never seen? Not only are you likely to picture the person incorrectly in your mind, but also you are listening to someone who is giving you fewer than half of the types of nonverbal signals you would receive in person. With E-mail, the message can become further distorted, because even basic signals such as tone of voice, vocal inflection, pitch, and timing are absent. Nonverbal communication helps in **clarifying mes-**

---

[1] Albert Mehrabian, *Nonverbal Communication* (Chicago: Atherton Company, 1972), pp. 23–38.

sages, allowing us to understand and interpret what the speaker means in the context in which it is being said. Context is a point of reference—a place from which to begin. When that context is absent, we are often left guessing.

3. Showing the speaker's reactions to the listener.   Next time you are a customer at a retail store, notice how the clerk—and the customers—use eye contact, facial expressions, tone and volume of voice, and other signals **showing reactions to the listener.** You might be surprised at how many different ways there are of saying things as simple as "hi" or "how are you," or even "Have a good day." Although the words are the same, variations in nonverbal signals are likely to show at least some differences in emotional reaction. These differences include variations in acceptance, approval, and comfort level.

BODY LANGUAGE

Body movements—of the arms, head, legs, and so on—are nonverbal communication channels. The general position of the body can give away attitudes toward other people, as well as toward oneself.[2] If someone leans toward you, for example, you can usually assume that he or she is expressing interest and a positive attitude. A slumped, shuffling body posture can be expressing feelings of low self-worth. **Body language** can also express differences in status. In a situation where status differences are likely to be felt (such as a staff meeting), those with the higher status positions will often assume a posture that is relaxed and "laid back." Those of lower status meanwhile are forced to show their tension with a less relaxed posture.[3]

TONE OF VOICE AND OTHER VOCAL CUES

Some nonverbals are transmitted through the voice. They include our **tone of voice,** volume, pauses, pitch, tone, and speed, among other factors. Take a look at the different ways the following sen-

---

[2] Ibid.

[3] See Erving Goffman, "The Nature of Deference and Demeanor," *American Anthropologist* 58 (1956), pp. 473–502.

tence can be understood based only on the differences in which words are emphasized:

John really enjoys eating pizza. (Even though other people might dislike pizza, John really likes it.)

John *really* enjoys eating pizza. (John's enjoyment seems to be greater than the enjoyment of others who eat pizza.)

John really enjoys *eating* pizza. (Although John might not like buying or cooking pizza, the eating part he likes.)

John really enjoys eating *pizza*. (Although he might dislike other foods, pizza is an exception.)

What thoughts are suggested to you when someone pauses for a long time before answering a question you have asked? Most of us would assume that the answer wasn't readily available to that person—that the person would have to search his or her memory for the answer. What about a very soft tone of voice as an answer to a question? Or very rapid talking? All of these are clues that can help us understand the whole message when we listen carefully. Notice that listening carefully involves more than simply hearing the words.

FACIAL EXPRESSION AND EYE CONTACT

Facial expressions show our emotions more clearly than they express anything else. The interpretation of these expressions are also more universal than any other nonverbal behavior, with the possible exception of vocal tone.[4] Ironically, we also try to deceive others more frequently with our facial expressions than with other nonverbal behaviors. Research also shows that most of us are better at deceiving others through facial expressions than through any other nonverbal signal.[5] Of course, when we are busy deceiving others

---

[4] Paul Ekman, "The Universal Smile: Face Muscles Talk Every Language," *Psychology Today,* April 1975, pp. 35–39.

[5] See Paul Ekman, Wallace V. Friesen, and Phoebe Ellsworth, "What Emotion Categories or Dimensions Can Observers Judge From Facial Behavior?" In P. Ekman, ed., *Emotion in The Human Face* (Cambridge, Eng: Cambridge University Press, 1982).

with our facial expressions, we might be betraying our true feelings in other ways.

When we examine eye contact between individuals, the most important factor is duration; that is, the length of time we spend looking into the eyes of the other person. A great deal of research has been done on this very subject; we will highlight only some of the more important findings here. First, people who use a great deal of eye contact are usually thought to be more attentive, more tuned in than others, however accurate that perception might be.

Another finding is the tendency to communicate by changing our level of eye contact. When we feel embarrassed or threatened by the other speaker or by something that has been said, we often look away, thus communicating that we need a change in the conversation.[6] We also tend to lower our gaze when we feel that others have invaded our personal space.[7] Eye contact also can show status differences, feelings of attraction or repulsion, and gender and race differences.[8] People tend to be drawn more toward us when we maintain a fairly high level of eye contact. This shows that we are interested both in the other person and in the conversation. However, be careful not to jump too quickly to conclusions about other people based on their facial expressions or eye contact.

DISTANCING

Another area of nonverbal communication is called distancing. Like animals, humans also have "territory." How much of this territory each of us needs varies from person to person and from ethnic group to ethnic group. No matter who we are, we all carry around a "bubble of space" (see Figure 15–1). Each "bubble" has its rules about who is invited into it. The first bubble—intimate distance—we reserve for those with whom we are intimate, such as significant others, *very* close friends, and our children. It extends from physical contact out to 18 inches or so. The next bubble, ex-

---

[6] R. J. Edelman and S. E. Hampson, "Embarrassment in Dyadic Interaction," *Social Behavior and Personality* 9 (1981), pp. 171–77.

[7] C. L. Kleinke, "Gaze and Eye Contact: A Research Review," *Psychological Bulletin* 100 (1986), pp. 78–100.

[8] Nancy M. Henley, *Body Politics: Power, Sex, and Nonverbal Communication* (New York: Simon & Schuster, 1986).

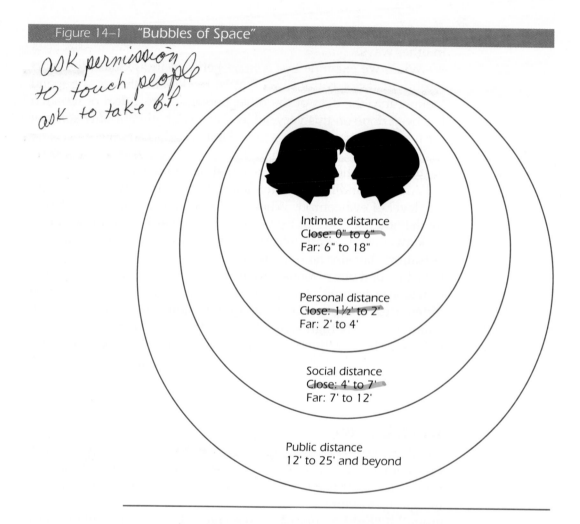

Figure 14–1   "Bubbles of Space"

[handwritten note:] ask permission to touch people / ask to take B.P.

Intimate distance
Close: 0" to 6"
Far: 6" to 18"

Personal distance
Close: 1½' to 2'
Far: 2' to 4'

Social distance
Close: 4' to 7'
Far: 7' to 12'

Public distance
12' to 25' and beyond

tending from about 18 inches out to four feet, is the personal distance we save for close friends. The third area of space—social distance—from about 4 feet to 12 feet, we use for communicating with business contacts and brief acquaintances. The last bubble—our public distance—from 12 feet on out, we use for the general public.[9]

_____
[9] See Edward T. Hall, "Proxemics—A Study of Man's Spatial Relationships," from *Man's Image in Medicine and Anthropology* (New York: International Universities Press, 1963).

When any of the first three bubbles is violated, we feel very uncomfortable. Even when Americans ride subways and crowded elevators every day of their lives, they never really get to like the daily violations of their personal space. Next time you are in a crowded public vehicle or elevator, notice the facial expressions of your fellow passengers. On most, you will see looks of resignation. They have accepted this invasion of their space as necessary, but most of us never come to like it.

Distancing varies between cultures. In some cultures, being very close to another person is much more acceptable than in the United States and most European cultures. For example, in the Arab world, two businessmen will typically stand about 18 inches from each other while talking about business. Most Far Eastern societies also feel more comfortable with strangers at close range than Americans. As the world becomes more of a global community, learning the distancing needs of other societies will become increasingly more important.

Key Terms

nonverbal
  behavior
nonverbal
  messages

three functions of
  nonverbals:
  showing emotion
  clarifying
    messages
  showing
    reactions to
    listener

body language
tone of voice
facial expressions
eye contact
distancing
"bubble of space"

Review Questions

1. How can a knowledge of nonverbal behavior help your human relations skills on the job?
2. Are nonverbal signals ever sent over the telephone? If so, which ones? Explain.
3. What types of messages have you received from the facial expressions of others?

4. In your daily life, how do the "bubbles of space" affect your overall communications with others?

5. How can the material in this chapter help you in dealing with customers or clients? with your manager?

Multiple Choice

1. Which of the following statements about nonverbal messages is *false?*
   a. Nonverbal messages show the speaker's feelings and emotions.
   b. Nonverbal messages always agree with the verbal messages.
   c. Nonverbal messages clarify spoken messages.
   d. Nonverbal messages show the speaker's reaction to others.

2. Body language:
   a. Includes movements of the arms, head, and legs.
   b. Provides no real clues as to meaning of a verbal message.
   c. Includes tone of voice and volume.
   d. Is something a speaker is always aware of.

3. The first "bubble of space" is the one we usually reserve for:
   a. Business associates.
   b. Friends and acquaintances.
   c. People with whom we are very intimate.
   d. The general public.

4. Which of the following is *not* a type of nonverbal communication?
   a. Tone of voice
   b. Facial expressions
   c. Overall meaning
   d. Body language.

5. The most important issue in examining eye contact between speakers is:
   a. Duration, that is, how long we look at the other person.
   b. Whether we're looking the other person in the eye or generally at the body.
   c. How often we blink during a conversation.
   d. How large the pupils of the eye become during a conversation.

3 points short

The "Defective" CD Player

Sherry Austin worked at the customer service desk of a megamarket. She and her co-workers were frequently told, "Your job is to turn a discontented customer into a happy one who will return here regularly." One evening Mrs. Celeni, an elderly customer, came in with a portable CD player. Her sales slip indicated it had been purchased only two days before. "I just need my money back," she said in a monotone. "Did it fail to work properly?" Sherry queried. "It's OK. I just need my money more than I need this thing," was the response. Sherry noticed, though, that Mrs. Celeni seemed to be showing signs of confusion and maybe even some frustration. If all the customer wanted was her money back because she had decided she didn't need a portable CD player, fine. But Sherry wasn't sure.

After asking more questions and observing nonverbal behavior that seemed to contradict what Mrs. Celeni was saying, Sherry finally discovered the real problem. The CD player was a little complicated, more so than most that the store sold. Mrs. Celeni had tried but couldn't get it to operate properly. Rather than blaming the product, she blamed herself. Not wanting to appear stupid, she had returned to the store for a refund. Once Sherry had established the problem, she quickly paged someone from the electronics department. In 10 minutes, the electronics salesperson had explained the way the player worked, and Mrs. Celeni decided to keep it. Before she left with her CD player, she thanked Sherry. "I really wanted this player. Thanks for all your help." Sherry whispered so nobody could hear, "Thanks for all of your nonverbals."

1. How has an awareness on nonverbal signals helped Sherry in her job as a customer service representative?

2. What if Sherry hadn't been able to find the real problem? How long should she probe for the real reasons before simply refunding the money as requested?

3. How could some training about nonverbal behavior help people in jobs like Sherry's?

15

Chapter

Learning to Communicate in Other Cultures

Kim, a 20-year-old Korean college student, is in Seattle visiting his American-born cousin, Sam, who is also 20 and in college. Since Sam doesn't speak Korean, and Kim speaks limited English, they haven't gotten to know each other very well. But they're taking this opportunity to do so.

"Sam, what are your career plans after college?" asks Kim.

"I don't know. I'll get a job in whatever I finally decide to major in, I guess, or maybe I'll just get a job wherever I decide to move to after college," says Sam.

Kim was shocked. "Wherever *you* decide to move? Whatever *you* decide to major in? I don't understand! My family at home has chosen my future job for me already! And I would *not* move away from them. They are too helpful to me!"

The world has become a smaller place these days, thanks to technology and increased mobility. Family members can easily move to another country, instead of only to another village as they might have a hundred years ago. The world is also increasingly becoming an international and intercultural workplace. Every year, more U.S. companies open offices overseas, while more foreign companies are opening offices in the United States. Experts predict that by the year 2000 about half of the world's assets will be held by multinational corporations.[1] This means that the odds are good that many of us will work for at least one of these globe-trotting organizations at some time in our work lives.

EXAMPLES OF INTERCULTURAL MISUNDERSTANDINGS

In families or in businesses, misunderstandings sometimes arise when people from different cultures don't understand each other. The following are some examples of problems that can happen. In Japan, giving small gifts is expected in most business situations, but in China, giving someone a gift in a business setting is not allowed. In most of Latin America, appointment times are not strictly kept, and most people arrive late at meetings; in Sweden, however, being on time is important. In the United States, to "table" a meeting agenda item means to put it off until later; in England, to "table" an item means to put it on the table, or talk about it right then. In Mexico, it is polite to ask about a customer's family, but in Saudi Arabia that would be considered rude.[2] In China, it is all right to stare at people, but in the United States that is considered rude. In some Arab countries, sitting cross-legged and "aiming" the sole of the shoe at someone is considered an insult; in the United States, it is not. And in several cultures, eating with the left hand is considered bad manners; in the United States, we don't mind.[3]

HIGH-CONTEXT AND LOW-CONTEXT CULTURES

Edward T. Hall describes different cultures as being high-context or low-context, which has to do with the **social context** that business agreements are made in.[4] In **high-context cultures,** the atmosphere

---

[1] Ronald E. Dulek, John S. Fielden, and John S. Hill, "International Communication: An Executive Primer," _Business Horizons_, Jan.–Feb. 1991, p. 20.

[2] Lennie Copeland, "Training Americans to do Business Overseas," _Training_, July 1993, p. 12.

[3] Dick Shaef, "The Growing Need for Cross-Cultural and Bilingual Training," _Training/Human Resource Director_, Jan. 1981, pp. 85–86.

[4] Edward T. Hall, _The Silent Language_ (Greenwich, CT: Fawcett Books, 1959), pp. 51–53.

surrounding communication is more important than the words written into a contract. Factors in the cultural atmosphere include, for example, the culture's norms or rules, nonverbal behaviors on both sides, and anything else that affects how people communicate. In a high-context culture, people have to be careful in their business communications, so that misunderstandings don't lead to a situation where people on either side come away with a different understanding of what they agreed to.

In **low-context cultures,** on the other hand, the written word itself is considered a binding contract. Contracts or business agreements in a low-context culture can be taken at face value, and the atmosphere or environment in which they are written is not important.

Examples of High-Context and Low-Context Cultures

Some examples of high-context cultures include Japan, the Arab countries, Latin American countries, and Italy. Some examples of low-context cultures include Germany, the Scandinavian countries, Canada, and the United States.

Communicating in High-Context Cultures

Most of us in the United States are familiar with low-context cultures, so we don't have trouble communicating with other low-context cultures. But what happens when we try to communicate with people in high-context cultures? Sometimes communication breaks down, causing problems or misunderstandings. Here are some suggestions for communicating with people from high-context cultures. They can be helpful in business transactions or in regular conversations.[5]

1. **Let others get to know you.** People in high-context cultures often need to know how to put you into context, so that they can understand you better. They need to know about you, about your company or organization, and even about your family background. Without an understanding of who you are, any business agreement you make could be meaningless.

---

[5] These four principles are based on Dulek, Fielden, and Hill, pp. 21–22.

2. Speak slowly and clearly. Avoid using slang terms, clichés, jargon, and so on. Nonnative English speakers often learn to speak English from a textbook, or from an instructor who also does not speak English as a first language. This means that they often do not learn informal expressions, and misunderstanding can occur. Informal language slips out even when we are unaware of it. Expressions such as "Let's run that idea up the flagpole and see if anyone salutes," may make perfect sense to you, but think about how this type of expression sounded to you the first time you heard it. Didn't you have to stop and figure it out?

3. Include words from your listener's native language. No one can be fluent in every language in the world, but when you know ahead of time that you are going to be talking to someone who is from a non–English-speaking country, prepare yourself. Sprinkle your conversation with at least a few words or expressions from their language. In most cultures, it is considered good manners to learn expressions from the other person's language. It shows you are interested and respectful enough to do a little learning. Of course, you must be careful that you understand what you are saying, and that you can pronounce the words and phrases so that they at least are recognizable!

4. Watch your nonverbal signals. Hand movements, gestures, posture, tone of voice, and even eye movements can send *nonverbal signals* that you don't know you are sending. If you are speaking to someone through a translator, and the listeners are listening for long periods of time without understanding your words, they are even more likely to pick up on your nonverbal signals.

You should find these suggestions helpful when you are communicating in high-context situations. But even when you are in a low-context situation, these suggestions will help you appear more thoughtful and will pay off in the end.

INDIVIDUALIST AND COLLECTIVIST CULTURES

Another way to think about how cultures are different is to look at how people in those cultures identify themselves and fulfill themselves. In some cultures, individual achievement and control is important, while in others, the needs of the social group are more important than those of the individual. Consider your own orientation by answering these questions, taken from the Individualism-Collectivism Scale developed by psychologist C. Harry Hui.[6]

1. I would help if a colleague at work told me that he or she needed money to pay utility bills.
2. Young people should take into consideration their parents' advice when making education or career plans
3. I am often influenced by the moods of my neighbors.

How did you answer these questions? Do you place more importance on individual goals and identity, or on whatever is good for the group?

Individualism

In the United States and other industrialized Western cultures, we usually place more value on *individualism*. In individualist cultures, being a rugged, self-reliant, and independent individual is considered important. We tend to admire and even glorify people who go out on their own and fulfill their own needs, rather than fulfilling the expectations of other people. American history books are filled with the names of people we now think of as heroes who went against the flow of the crowd and succeeded because of it—Abraham Lincoln, Henry Ford, Theodore Roosevelt, Eleanor Roosevelt, Daniel Boone, Jane Addams, Susan B. Anthony, Thomas Edison, Martin Luther King, Jr., and Douglas MacArthur, to name a few. The United States is considered a land of opportunity, a land where anyone who works hard enough can succeed. The key idea is *anyone* can succeed on his or her own. Success is viewed as each individual's task. Even movie stars who seem to be rugged individualists become idols—James Dean (who is honored on a postage stamp) and John Wayne (who is also on a postage stamp and has an airport named after him in Orange County, California).

Individualism is more often found in affluent cultures, areas with easy mobility, urban areas, and exposure to the mass media.[7]

---

[6] C. Harry Hui, "Measurement of Individualism-Collectivism," *Journal of Research in Personality* 22, 1988, pp. 17–36).

[7] Harry C. Triandis et al, "An Etic-Emic Analysis of Individualism and Collectivism," *Journal of Cross-Cultural Psychology* 24 (1993) pp. 366–83.

Collectivism

Asian countries and Third World countries tend to place more value on *collectivism.* In collectivist cultures, priority is given to the good of the group—the family, village, clan, or work group—and not to the individual group member. In these cultures, books and movies glorify and celebrate people who resist the temptation to be self-indulgent, and instead, remember their place in society and wind up being dutiful to the group. Take an Asian expression: "The nail that stands out will be pounded down." In this expression, a person who tries to be an individual will feel the pressure of the group to become part of the group. And from another collectivist culture, Africa, comes the saying, "It takes a whole village to raise a child."

Collectivism is more often found in cultures where people are not affluent, where they face threats from famine or natural disasters, where families are large, and where cooperation is required to survive (such as harvesting crops or building villages).[8]

INDIVIDUALISM, COLLECTIVISM, AND SELF-CONCEPT

People in individualist cultures have their own identity outside of their family, friends, or work group. Therefore, they feel freer to leave homes, jobs, churches, and communities to look for better opportunities. As they enter adulthood, they struggle to find their own separate identity. But in collectivist cultures, extended families are closer knit, and the family and larger social network help a person define who he or she is. In many languages, a person's family name is written first (Chu Ken instead of Ken Chu), which emphasizes the person's family and social identity. Even commercials and advertisements in collectivist cultures emphasize the good of the group—for example, a product might be advertised to "bring people closer together," whereas in individualist cultures an ad for the same product might promise to give someone "a new look all your own."

---

[8] Harry Triandis et al, 366–83.

INTERACTING IN DIFFERENT CULTURES

Individualists who visit collectivist cultures may be able to avoid misunderstandings and awkwardness by avoiding confrontation, trying to cultivate relationships over the long term instead of expecting to be instant friends, being modest, and paying attention to people's positions or social status. Collectivists who visit individualist cultures should feel more free to criticize something they think is wrong, get right down to business without formalities, be open about their own skills and accomplishments, and pay more attention to personal attitudes than to group memberships and positions.[9]

Knowing a person's social identity is important in all kinds of cultures. In some cultures, though, a person's most important identity is the group while in other cultures, the person's membership in the group is not as important as his or her own individuality.

Key Terms

social context

high-context cultures

low-context cultures

individualist cultures

collectivist cultures

Review Questions

1. We live in a mostly individualist culture. Think about the country where your family originated, regardless of how many generations ago it may have been. Would you consider that country more individualist or collectivist? Why?

2. Most of us don't give much thought to the importance of nonverbal signals, especially in low-context cultures. To see how important the nonverbal signal of voice tone is, try this

---

[9] Harry C. Triandis, R. Brislin, and C. H. Hui, "Cross-Cultural Training across the Individualism-Collectivism Divide," *International Journal of Intercultural Relations* 12 (1988), pp. 269–89.

quick exercise. Say the phrase, "That was really funny," in an alternatively sincere, sarcastic, angry, and bored tone of voice.

3. In which country would your family background become important during a job interview, the United States or Japan? Why?

4. One of the suggestions for communicating in high-context cultures is that you learn words or phrases from other languages. Make a list (written or oral) of all the foreign words or phrases that you already know, especially "thank you," "please," "hello," and "goodbye." Are you surprised by how long the list is?

5. In the opening story, Sam and Kim were related, they were the same age, and they were both college students. What made their experiences so different from each other?

Multiple Choice

1. Your supervisor tells you to ignore everything about a client except his signature on the dotted line. What kind of culture does your supervisor represent?
   a. High-context
   b. Low-context
   c. Medium-context
   d. Social-context

2. You are riding on the bus across town, and you strike up a conversation with a stranger. Within minutes, you know all about the person's company and family, but not much about the person's personality, or his or her likes or dislikes. What kind of culture is this person probably from?
   a. High-context
   b. Low-context
   c. Medium-context
   d. Social-context

3. Suggestions for communicating in high-context cultures include:
   a. Conceal information about yourself.
   b. Speak casually, using informal words and phrases.
   c. Sprinkle your conversation with words from the listener's native language.
   d. Ignore nonverbal signals that you send or receive.

4. Experts predict that by the year 2000:
   a. The United States will hold more than half of the world's assets.
   b. Multinational corporations will hold more than half of the world's assets.
   c. Small countries alone will hold more than half of the world's assets.
   d. The world will end.
5. Which of the following proverbs is most likely to be found in an individualist culture?
   a. "It takes a whole village to raise a child."
   b. "The nail that stands out gets pounded down."
   c. "The wheel that squeaks gets the grease."
   d. "A round peg can't fit into a square hole."

Case 15–1

The Case of "Classroom Hollywood"

Lisa Sorensen had been teaching college classes for years in southern California. She also was actively involved in her two teenaged sons' lives. Expressions she learned from her sons often crept into her lectures, which usually wasn't a problem because most of her students were about the age of her kids and understood what she meant.

In addition to using some slang, Lisa often ended classes by saying "OK, that's a wrap." Many of her students were taking classes to prepare for careers in the entertainment industry, but most students in other majors also knew this was a filmmaking expression which here meant that class was over. On the first day of class in a new term, Lisa ended class early with her usual expression. As students filed out of the room, she noticed looks of panic appear on the faces of two Japanese exchange students, Masao and Kimiko. They whispered to each other for a few moments, then approached Lisa and asked to speak with her privately.

"We are very sorry, but we cannot remain in your class," Masao told her gravely. "You speak a much different English than we have learned in school. Much faster, too. We do not understand much of what you say." With that, they left the room. Lisa was dumbfounded. "What did I say?" she wondered.

1. What is the basic communication problem between Lisa and her foreign exchange students in the story?

2. In the story above, who is from a high-context culture and who is from a low-context culture? Who is from a collectivist culture and who is from an individualist culture?

3. Consider some of the suggestions for learning to communicate with people from high-context cultures. What could Lisa do differently in her classes for the next term?

16

Watch for Hidden Agendas

Kate Sawyer, Felix Rodriguez, and Kelvin Campbell were sitting in their company's conference room one Wednesday afternoon. They were waiting for the rest of the Company Employees Morale Improvement Committee members to arrive so that their weekly meeting could start.

Kate: You know, Kelvin, I never figured you for someone who was that interested in company improvement. Why were you so interested in joining this committee?

Kelvin: Well . . . can you keep a secret? [*whispering*] I really don't give a darn about company morale or efficiency or anything else, but my supervisor told me that doing some committee work would help me get my next promotion. What about you? Why are you here?

Kate: [*laughing*] That's pretty funny, because the only reason I'm here is to get away from my desk for a couple of hours a week. I don't care about this committee work, either!

Felix: You two are unbelievable! Who needs a regular meeting agenda, with all these hidden agendas going on!

What do we mean by hidden agendas? How do hidden agendas hurt groups and organizations? In this chapter, we will be discussing this special type of problem that makes groups ineffective. We will also talk about some other barriers to group effectiveness, such as poor group makeup, lack of creativity, conflict in the group, one-member domination, resisting change, norms and rules that don't work, and other problems.

HIDDEN AGENDAS

Have you ever been part of a group that just didn't seem to get anything done? Hidden agendas may have been to blame. Hidden agendas are the secret wishes, hopes, desires, and assumptions that members don't want to share with the group. Members may try to get their hidden agendas accomplished at the same time they pretend to care about the goals of the group.

Getting Rid of Hidden Agendas

Hidden agendas don't just happen within other people. You need to consider your own hidden agendas and get rid of them before thinking about the hidden agendas of the other people in a group. Before you sit down in a group, sit down alone and ask yourself, "What do I want from this group? What do I expect? Can I make sure my personal needs don't block my judgment in this group?"

An even harder job than getting rid of your own personal agendas is to try to get rid of the hidden agendas of other people, so the group's performance isn't damaged. If you are the leader of the group, you have enough power to prevent people's agendas from hurting the group. Even as a group member who is not the leader, you can help by watching your own behaviors and those of other group members. Here are some suggestions for doing so.

1. **Watch for strong emotions in others.** What are the emotions based on? Is the group member afraid of something? Is the group member jealous? Is the hidden agenda based on a prejudice or bias that is threatened by whatever is on the real agenda? For example, someone who has been a member of a committee for a long time may feel jealous about a new member who joins the group and then starts making a lot of decisions for the group. The long-term member may feel that he or she is losing power to the new member.

2. **Watch for contradictions between what people say and how they act.** You may be able to figure out hidden agendas through gestures, eye contact, head nodding, and body movements. For example, a group member may say in a meeting, "Yes, I think we should try to raise money for an employee-sponsored college scholarship," while at the same time, the person is sitting with arms folded across his chest, frowning, and shaking his head. Does he really like the idea of the scholarship, or not?

3. **Watch for themes that keep coming up after the topic was changed.** These recurring themes, or hidden agenda topics, may be disguised. If this hidden agenda is a deeply felt or personal issue to the group member, it could become an underlying issue in any group discussion. For example, a group member may feel strongly that new safety procedures need to be started at the company. She feels strongly about this issue, but she finds that every time the topic comes up, it is dismissed. So she continues to bring it up, waiting for the group to take some interest in it.

4. **Watch for agenda conflicts that threaten a member's self-esteem.** These are sometimes the easiest issues to spot. Self-esteem issues are usually behind all or part of hidden agenda issues. The group member may feel that his or her personal self-esteem is somehow competing with the esteem of the group as a whole. For example, a group member may have come to the group with a new idea for an employee recognition program. She really wants this program to be started, but the group votes against it. She starts to feel that their no votes are personal rejections and that her personal self-esteem is at stake. She keeps pushing the program, and the group keeps rejecting it, a competition that damages the group.

MEETING BEFORE OR AFTER THE MEETING

Sometimes a few group members agree on a hidden agenda for a group's purpose and goals. Or they may have their own ideas about how the group should be run. Agreements among these few members are made away from the rest of the group, so this smaller subgroup comes into the group meeting with its goals and plans in place. Subgroups can be hard to spot. In this case, it is up to the group leader to take a "time-out" during the meeting of the whole group to bring everyone back together by reminding the group that decisions will be made only during the meeting and by the group as a whole.

POOR GROUP MAKEUP

Sometimes a group is made up of members who lack the skills or the knowledge to make the group work effectively. It is not always possible to get new group members or to remove old members. In this case, the group members will have to do "homework" to get up to speed and help the group work effectively. They may have to change the group makeup by bringing in former group members to help out as consultants. They may even need to hire outside consultants to help the group focus and to figure out what they should be doing.

For example, let's assume that a rural area has just been awarded a grant to start a youth services program. A board of directors will have to be recruited from interested people in the community to get the group going. The board members will need to get some direction about their responsibilities. They can contact public relations firms in the area to find someone who is willing to volunteer time to come to a board meeting as an outside consultant. This public relations firm helps the board to identify its goals: raise money and inform the community about the youth services program. Now the board is able to begin to work effectively to get the program going successfully.

A group that is changed to include people with the best skills and knowledge available will grow. There may be some growing pains, just as any new group has to adjust. The leader has to be able to help out in this readjustment process.

WHEN GROUP RULES OR NORMS DON'T WORK

Most groups never talk about their norms or hidden rules. The result is that groups sometimes have ineffective group norms or rules that don't work or that may even hurt the group's performance. For example, each member of the group may have a different idea about the goals of the group and how they should be accomplished because these goals were never discussed in the beginning. In this case, the group leader's job is to get the group as a whole to agree on the purpose of the group, the role of each member in achieving that purpose, and the need for changing certain norms or hidden rules. For example, a group norm that was never discussed might be something as simple as punctuality. Let's say a work group decides to meet from 1:00–3:00 PM every Monday. The leader may be operating on the rule or norm (never discussed) that the group will meet until all the necessary work is done or all the agenda items have been discussed and resolved, even if that means going past 3:00 PM. But other group members may be operating under the understanding that the group will stop meeting at 3:00 PM, even if all items haven't been discussed or the work isn't finished, and will pick up unfinished items at the next meeting. So around 3:00 PM, when people start shuffling in their seats or begin trickling out of the meeting, the group leader doesn't understand why. This can cause confusion and hostility among group members.

CONFLICT AMONG GROUP MEMBERS

Sometimes group members don't get along, for whatever reason but usually because they bring some past history into the work group or meeting. When conflict among group members happens, it doesn't matter what issue is being discussed in the group because one member of the group will try to make another member look bad, or will disagree just to disagree, and the group will not be productive. Depending on the seriousness of the conflicts or how disruptive they are to the group, the leader must decide how to reduce conflicts between members. For example, the group leader may have to pull them aside away from the group and say, "Look, Steve, I know you think Kaylor beat you out of a promotion last year. Kaylor, I know you think Steve has been talking badly about you behind your back. That's between the two of you. While you are both in this group, I need you to act like responsible adults and work together on this project. If you can't do that, tell me now, and I'll get someone else to work on this project."

In some cases, the conflict may not be between individual members but between competing groups. For example, the marketing department of an advertising agency may have to meet regularly with the design and production department. Secretly, each group thinks the other doesn't pull its weight and doesn't work very hard. The members of each group may try to sabotage the other group by voting for or working on issues that will help or make their own group look good. In this case, again, it is up to the leader to pull them together. This will probably mean bringing the issue out into the open at a work session where everyone must talk about it and agree to work together as a unit.

LACK OF CREATIVITY IN THE GROUP

Some groups don't get anywhere because they have a lack of creativity. Group members can't think of creative solutions to problems. If groups take time to do exercises such as brainstorming, they can increase their creativity. Businesses have used brainstorming a great deal for many years. The process has specific rules. First, an issue is introduced for workers to talk about. Everyone then has the job of thinking of creative solutions, no matter how bizarre the ideas may be. Ideas should build on each other, and no criticism of ideas is allowed. After the brainstorming session, group members may have a large number of possible solutions to choose from.

ONE-MEMBER DOMINATION

Many groups are dominated by one member, who may be the group leader or someone from the group who thinks he or she has the best ideas. When one-member domination occurs, the group leader can reduce the dominator's talking time by asking everyone individually for ideas and giving everyone equal time to talk. The leader may have to take the dominating person aside and point out the behavior. "Darla, I know you think you have the best answers about how to solve these problems, but I'd like you to give other people time to talk, too. It's important that we hear from everybody." In some cases, the person who is dominating meetings may not even realize it.

When it's the group leader who is doing all the talking, the rest of the group will have a harder time reducing the dominating. But if group members agree to reducing it, they can tell the leader that *everyone's* ideas should have a chance to be heard.

RESISTANCE TO CHANGE

Both individuals and groups as a whole may have a hard time doing things differently than they've been done before. If you ask them why they want things done a certain way, the answer is most likely to be "because that's the way we've always done it." This resistance to change goes along with that old saying, "If it ain't broke, don't fix it." The increase in technology has brought about change everywhere in how groups operate and communicate. The group leader may have to tell the group that change is inevitable. For example, "We're going to try this new computer on-line customer registration process. We think it will save the company about a week of typing in the information, and we'll be able to keep better records. I know there will be bugs, but our job will be to work them out."

OTHER PROBLEMS

Some groups get stalled or don't work well together for reasons that the group can't figure out. Members should discuss how they can contribute to the work project, so that all of their abilities are used to the maximum. New job assignments could be given so that all members will feel they are contributing and using their individual talents and skills in the process.

 ## Key Terms

hidden agendas

recurring themes

group makeup

ineffective group
  norms or rules

conflict among
  group members

lack of creativity

one-member
  domination

resistance to
  change

Review Questions

1. How do hidden agendas hurt groups or organizations? Give some examples of causes of hidden agendas.
2. How do lack of creativity and resistance to change hurt a group's effectiveness? Could these two problems be related?
3. Have you ever been in a group that didn't work well, and you wondered how the members got into the group in the first place? How can problems from poor group makeup be reduced?
4. What would you say to a person who interrupted and took over every discussion in a group? How can one-member domination be reduced by changing the group rules or norms?
5. After reading this chapter, imagine that you are in charge of setting up "ground rules" for a new work group. What would you include?

Multiple Choice

1. Which of the following actions would be best to take when the group is made up of people who don't really fit the group's needs:
   a. Remove members whose skills don't fit the group.
   b. Bring members "up to speed."
   c. Bring in new members who have the right knowledge.
   d. All of the above might work, depending on the situation.
2. How can you tell if a group member has a hidden agenda?
   a. Watch for agenda conflicts that involve a member's self-esteem.
   b. Watch for lack of emotions when issues are discussed.
   c. Watch for themes that come up once and then are dropped.
   d. Watch for similarity between verbal and nonverbal signals.
3. How can group norms or rules be made more effective?
   a. The group's leader gets the group members to agree on the roles each member can play in achieving the group's purpose.
   b. Each member decides alone what the purpose of the group is.

c. The group agrees not to discuss their hidden goals.

    d. The group leader gets the group to agree that their rules or norms don't need to be changed.

4. Which of the following choices are *not* reasons why groups lose their effectiveness:

    a. Lack of creativity and resistance to change.

    b. Conflict among members and one-person domination.

    c. Loss of groupthink and getting rid of mindguards.

    d. Ineffective group norms or hidden rules and hidden agendas.

5. Which of the following behaviors breaks a rule about brainstorming:

    a. Tina says to Roger, "That was the stupidest idea I ever heard of."

    b. Raimundo says to James, "How about using the colors you suggested for the logo symbol in part of the title, too!"

    c. Rachelle says to the group, "Let's allow an hour for this session. No idea is too bizarre."

    d. Morgan says to Danielle, "Wow, I never would have thought of that, but it just might work!"

Case 16–1

What's the Real Agenda?

Menandro Cunanan is the director of a small hospital supplies firm. The president has assigned him to get a group of employees together to work on improving employee relations in the firm. He now has three other employees who have agreed to work with the group. Today, they are meeting for the first time. After the meeting is called to order we observe the following conversation:

Fred Smith: Well, I've been saying it for years, I just don't think we need to have any more administrators. This company would run a lot better if it weren't so top-heavy. Maybe now someone will listen to me.

Tess Flores: Are you talking about me? After all, I'm the newest administrator. You're making me feel kind of bad here.

Meanwhile, Lyle O'Neal just smiles and nods energetically at everything that is said.

Menandro sighs and thinks to himself, "I've got my work cut out for me, getting this group to work together."

1. Do Fred, Tess, and Lyle have any hidden agendas? If so, what are they? How can you tell?

2. What steps could Menandro take to set up some rules for the group's purpose and how it is going to work?

3. If Menandro doesn't do anything to get this group on track, what other barriers to group effectiveness could you see arising with this particular group?

17

How to Get Rid of the Games People Play— Including Your Own

The setting is a busy insurance office. Judy walks over to Juanita's desk and asks her, "Would you mind finishing this financial report for me? I'm really swamped, and it's almost finished. Just needs a couple more hours." Juanita hesitates. "Besides," Judy continues, "when it's done, you can put your name on it and present it to the board of directors at their next meeting. You'll get a lot of credit for being on the ball. After all, the request was for someone in this department to do the report, not necessarily me." "OK," Juanita finally replies, "I guess I can find the time." A few hours later when Juanita examines the report more carefully, she realizes that it will require at least two days of full-time work to complete it meaningfully.

Juanita has just become the victim of a workplace game called bear trapper. The idea is to set the bait, making a tough job look really easy. Then, when the victim gives in, "Bang!" goes the bear trap. This is only one of dozens of identifiable games played daily in the workplaces of this world. Game playing wastes time, energy, morale, and money.

Game playing is making events and attitudes in the workplace appear different than they are, so that the player who starts them can get some type of payoff. A payoff is the reward that gives a feeling of temporary triumph to the person who starts the game. When trying to identify games, look for two important focal points: (1) Is this something that seems to happen over and over again? (2) Is there a payoff? If so, who is getting it?

COMMON GAMES PLAYED IN THE WORKPLACE

Bosses play games with employees. Employees play them with each other. And workers even start them with managers. The payoff is often nothing more sophisticated than a feeling that one person has gotten the better of the other. The payoffs themselves are rarely constructive; they often lead to further damaged human relations. Let's look at a few of the more common games played in the workplace.

Now I've Got You

Like bear trapper, now I've got you is an entrapment game, designed to trap people against their will. However, this game is different because the payoff involves catching the other person in a lie, mistake, or some other bad situation. When players succeed in trapping the victim, they usually feel justified in hurting the victim in some way—with an insult, a withheld favor, or even physical harm.

Tony finds an original document that Jane, another employee, has left in the department copy machine. It's an important legal release needed by a customer. State law requires that the original be submitted.

Tony: Hey, Jane, where's the original of that release you were copying?

Jane: It's on my my desk. Oh! [*looking quickly through both "in" and "out" baskets*] I can't find it.

> **Tony:** Well, come over to my desk; you might find it there. You are *so* forgetful!

Tony's payoff is feeling superior—for the time being—by having caught someone else in a minor mistake.

Why Don't You . . . Yes, But

Here is a conversation between two co-workers, Jerry, a secretary, and Elsie, a receptionist.

> **Jerry:** Elsie, the fax machine is jamming again.
>
> **Elsie:** Well, why don't you fix it?
>
> **Jerry:** I would, but I really don't know how.
>
> **Elsie:** Well, why don't you call the company that made the fax and ask how it can be unjammed in a case like this?
>
> **Jerry:** That's a good idea, but that's a long distance call, which I would have to get authorization for first, and the boss is gone.
>
> **Elsie:** Well, why don't you ask the maintenance department for help?
>
> **Jerry:** I would, but I just saw their supervisor a minute ago. They're all really busy right now.
>
> **Elsie:** Face it; you don't want to fix the fax machine.

Does this game sound familiar? It is common not only in the workplace, but also in many other situations. Have you ever been at a committee meeting where the chairperson was asking for constructive suggestions, but did not really accept any suggestions that were offered? Have you ever had an instructor who asked students for input on how a class should be run, only to go ahead and do what he or she had planned from the start? The payoff on **"why don't you . . . yes, but"** is for the player (pretending to listen carefully) to reassure both himself and the other, "Nobody's going to tell me what to do."

Kick Me

This game is played by a person whose actions are such that he or she might as well wear a sign that reads "Don't kick me." The temptation is hard to resist, and most people wouldn't have thought of doing any "kicking" had the person's attitude—the "sign"—not made them think of it. The kick me player also seems to express himself a lot in terms of WAHM ("Why [does this] Always Happen [to] Me?") If this game player happens to be surrounded by kind, warmhearted people who won't even respond to the "sign," his or her behavior will often become increasingly worse, until finally even the most polite person will oblige and give a swift kick.[1] The payoff in this game is actually negative, but the player's need is still fulfilled by it: The player somehow needs to confirm that he or she is bad and deserves a kick.

Blemish

This a true trivia game. For example, a restaurant manager spends most of his time checking inventory and other cost-related matters. He looks carefully for any contradictions in his employees' reports. When he finds one, he has discovered "proof"—a "blemish"—of the worthlessness of either whole projects or employees.[2] This game is a petty time waster. The payoff to the player is a temporary boost to his or her ego. "Detail persons" who feel that they aren't good at much else really like playing blemish.

Wooden Leg

This game is also known as "My Excuses Are Better than Yours." Excuses are the focus in wooden leg. Time, illness, childhood poverty—all are useful as excuses for whatever might go wrong. The player is like someone who says, "I can't walk very well because I have a wooden leg." An example might be this conversation between a manager and a sales executive:

Manager:	What's the matter, John? You're way behind on contacting those companies we were talking about for potential convention business.
Sales executive:	Well, Mr. Garcia, you know how tough it is to make contact with these firms. Monday

---

[1] Eric Berne, *Games People Play* (New York: Grove Press, 1964), pp. 84–85.

[2] Maurice F. Villere, Thomas S. O'Connor, and William J. Quain, "Games Nobody Wins: Transactional Analysis for the Hospitality Industry," *Cornell University HRA Quarterly* (Nov. 1983), p. 75.

is out because they're catching up with the weekend accumulation, and you can't call early in the morning because they're trying to wind up the previous day's business.[3]

Real excuses exist, but wooden leg makes an art of their use. One classic example is the bank teller who continues to make errors. When her manager asks what she thinks is wrong, the bank teller replies, "Well, you know, in the inner city school I went to, they didn't teach us math too well."

RAPO

In this game, the main player sets other people up, then slashes them once they are hooked. Like bear trapper and now I've got you, RAPO is an entrapment game. It is usually played between the sexes. At an office party, Jane walks up to Jim and this conversation takes place:

> **Jane:** Gee, I've been having a lot of trouble with those liability contracts I've been working on.
>
> **Jim:** I've been working with liability issues for a couple of years now [*which Jane already knew*], maybe I could give you a hand.
>
> **Jane:** Well, I don't think we could get together during work hours.
>
> **Jim:** You could come by my place after work, then.
>
> **Jane:** [*Yelling*] What kind of woman do you think I am?

The payoff in this instance is that Jim pays attention to Jane, while Jane doesn't have to give anything in the process. The game is an attention-getter that also can be played in a nonsexual context. It is often difficult to tell a RAPO player from a sincere, objective person, and it is almost always difficult to tell a RAPO player from someone who really wants romantic contact or needs help with work.[4]

---

[3] Ibid., p. 77.

[4] Eric Berne, *Beyond Games and Scripts* (New York: Random House, 1976), pp. 102–3.

Harried Worker

This game is played by someone who uses being "too busy" as an excuse not to interact with others. Three co-workers come by Brad's office and invite him to go out to "that new French place" for lunch. Brad protests that he's "just too busy to get away." The truth is that Brad wants to avoid the friendship of his fellow workers. People might have a variety of reasons for this type of payoff, in this case not wanting to get close to others; but usually the reason is related to low self-esteem.

HOW TO STOP THE GAMES

These are just a few of the games that are common in the workplace. Your knowledge of these, though, should help you with the two steps to identify game playing when you see it. *Recognition* is the first step. Most important, though, is the second step: *refusing to play.* Games require two players; if you refuse to play, there is no real game. Some additional steps you can take to reduce the game playing in your workplace are as follows:

1. **Work on building your self-esteem.** Low self-esteem is the single most important reason why people play games and allow themselves to be pulled into games by others. You also can get other people to play fewer games by doing and saying things that will help *their* self-esteem.

2. **Spend as much time as possible acting the part of an adult.** Games are not played by people who practice adult behavior. The adult part of our personality examines situations and people objectively, without knee jerk reaction or undue emotionality. To use this part of your personality, ask "how" questions, not "why" questions. Try to detach yourself from the emotional part of game playing that so often gets people hooked into playing the game all the way through to its completion.

3. **Get the other person to act as an adult.** Just as you are trying to act the part of an adult, lead the would-be game player down the same path. When the game player starts to talk to you like a selfish child or as a demanding parent, say something like, "Please explain that point a bit further; what do you mean by (whatever was said)."

4. **Give and receive "positive strokes" as often as practical.** In

Chapter 23, we will deal more with the idea of positive strokes. To put it simply, a **positive stroke is** an action or comment designed to make others feel good about themselves and their performance. A great deal of game playing is based on negatives. Getting rid of those negatives is also a good way to get rid of games.

5. **Avoid emphasizing the weaknesses of other people.**   All of us have weaknesses. By spending more time and energy noticing peoples' positive points, you can avoid the desire for payoffs—the unhealthy desire that urges us to play games in the first place.

If you are a manager, you can take positive steps to discourage game playing among your employees. Create a climate where people see game playing for what it is—a waste of time. We often play games because we are bored. Managers can do a lot to reduce boredom on the job by using devices such as job rotation, job enlargement, and job enrichment. Most important, a manager should allow people to work up to their full potential, so that they get a sense of fulfillment from the work they are doing.

If you are an employee, you can do many of the same things in a less formal way. With a positive attitude, you can create a mini-environment in your sector of the workplace—one that will discourage the games people play.

Key Terms

bear trapper	kick me	two steps to identify game playing
game playing	blemish	
payoff	wooden Leg	
now I've got you	RAPO	adult behavior
why don't you? . . . yes, but	harried worker	positive stroke

Review Questions

1. What is a game, and how can you usually tell when a game is being played?
2. Have you ever played a game at work or somewhere else? If so, who started it? What was the payoff?

3. Can you identify with any of the games mentioned in this chapter? Which one is most often played in your environment?
4. How does game playing hurt a company or other organization? Give examples.
5. List the rules on ending games and show how you would apply each one in a real-life situation.

Multiple Choice

1. People who start games, nearly always do so because they want a:
   a. Chance to get to the top of the corporate ladder.
   b. Payoff.
   c. Sexual encounter.
   d. Compliment.
2. A clerk has been caught giving incorrect change to customers several times in one morning. When confronted by her supervisor, she answers, "Well, I'm really sorry, but they didn't teach me much math in the little country school I went to." She is playing the game called:
   a. Why don't you . . . yes, but.
   b. RAPO
   c. Wooden Leg.
   d. Blemish.
3. Jim tells Sally, a classmate, "If you ever need wheels, just come on over to my place; I've got two cars, and I always hide the keys under the visor. Just help yourself." One day, a week later, Sally's own car breaks down a few blocks from Jim's house. She borrows the car to go get help. When she brings it back, Jim screams at her and calls her a car thief. What game has Jim been playing?
   a. Blemish
   b. RAPO
   c. Harried executive
   d. Wooden leg
4. Which of the following is an effective way to end game playing?
   a. Refuse to give the player the payoff he or she is seeking.
   b. Refuse to talk to the other person, who will soon decide that game playing isn't worth the struggle.

    c. Look the player in the eye and tell him or her to get lost.

    d. Start your own game to throw the player off the track.

5. Which of the following is *not* one of the strategies for stopping games in the workplace?

    a. Work on building your self-esteem.

    b. Avoid emphasizing the weakness of other people.

    c. Always use a steady and consistent eye contact when talking to others.

    d. Give and receive "positive strokes" as often as practical.

Case 17–1

The Weekly Meeting

J. R. Nelson runs a small furniture factory that employs about 100 people. The company has been in existence for 12 years with growing success, but the past six months have been slow. Each Friday morning, J. R. gets together with his managers and asks their advice. However, he listens briefly to every suggestion and then dismisses it for some reason. A typical meeting goes like this:

Nelson: Well, you all know how bad our situation is. Have any of you thought of some suggestions about what we can do to stop this downward trend?

Manager No. 1: What if we eliminate one of our three shifts and try to get more production out of the other two?

Nelson: Yes, that would cut our wage expenses down, but the union has always fought any change in our shift structure.

Manager No. 2: What about eliminating some of our territories, like the Pacific Northwest where the furniture isn't selling well, and put more energy into others areas.

Nelson: The Northwest has really fallen, all right, but we still need Seattle—can't eliminate that territory.

Manager No. 3:   What about using that new polyurethane filler for our upholstered furniture. It's supposed to be about half as expensive as what we're using.

Nelson: That's a good idea, but what will happen to our quality standards if we start changing our materials?

This type of dialogue goes on for about an hour, at which time Nelson thanks them all for their input and asks them to "keep thinking of new ideas. We'll see you here next Friday." Each week, the entire group becomes more frustrated. "Why doesn't he ever take our suggestions?" everyone asks. Meanwhile, productivity and morale continue to fall at the factory.

1. What game is J. R. Nelson playing with his managers? How can you identify it as a game?
2. What specific steps should the seven managers take to get this game to stop?
3. What is likely to happen to this furniture company if the situation continues for another six months?

18

Don't Let Those Workplace Changes Get You Down

Tonia has had a tough month. During the past three weeks, her department has been divided into five-member work teams. This week, the entire communication system in the company has been switched to E-mail, and next week her team has to learn an entirely new computerized bookkeeping system. "All these changes are making my head spin," she tells a co-worker. "Sometimes I find myself feeling that I'm not even working for the same company."

Tonia is not alone. In today's workplace, change is a way of life. How do you feel about change? If you're like most people, you have mixed feelings. Even when changes are obviously good for us and for our company, most of us still find that it has an unpleasant element. Many of us resist change without realizing why we are doing so.

Until about two centuries ago, people usually experienced a minimal amount of change during a lifetime. Death and disease took their toll, sometimes causing widespread and devastating changes in people's lives. But the regular, almost predictable changes in technology, social mores, and ways of life are a new part of today's reality. Since it's not realistic to try to prevent this inevitable change or to run away from it, we all need a strategy for coping.

In Chapter 9, we dealt with controlling the effects of stress. Change has been called the most universal stressor in the workplace. What are some practical steps we can take to minimize the impact of change on our personal and professional lives? Before we answer that question, let's look at the reasons—legitimate and otherwise—why we object to change.

RESISTANCE TO CHANGE

Human opposition is nearly always the major force of resistance to change. People resist change for a number of reasons. First, the status quo, or the way things already are, is too comfortable. Why should we get out of our comfort zone and try something new? It's a more secure feeling to know exactly what we're going to do each day.

1. **Individual perceptions of what is real.**   We all create a world based on our **perceptions of reality**. Once that world has been built, it resists change. We often choose how we hear and see data. Thus, we ignore information that challenges the stable world we have created. If a worker has a perception of reality that is threatened by the introduction of any change, that worker might hear and see the arguments for change in a negative way.

2. **Fear of the unknown.**   As we often find in the study of human relations, fear is everywhere. What we do or refuse to do is influenced by fear, but most of us won't admit this. Me, afraid? No, I just can't see why we need a change right now; that's all. Before you started studying this course, you probably had no real feeling for what the course would be like. You couldn't paint a mental picture of a typical class period and put yourself in it. That was just a bit unsettling, wasn't it? Obviously the **fear of the unknown** didn't overwhelm you, because here you are. However, fear of the unknown does overwhelm some people and serves as a major barrier to change organizationwide.

3. **Fear of loss.**   Many people dislike the thought of a major change at work because they fear for their jobs. A few years ago,

when computerization was new, the rumor mills churned out stories about people losing their jobs to computers. Few of the stories were true. The fear of loss also includes loss of status. "Maybe I won't be able to learn to operate a computer, and I'll be given a lesser job" could have been the cry of a frightened person in the early 1980s. The possibility of loss is nearly always exaggerated.

4. **Resentment toward the change agent.**   The person who is responsible for an organizational change is known as a change agent. Sometimes, people resist change because of feelings of resentment toward the change agent. Thus, an effective change agent must know to combat hostility and distrust and to build good relations and credibility with the people who will be affected by the change. Leadership must be effective or the change will fail.[1] Also, when facing change, make sure that your own objections are not focused on the change agent.

5. **Belief that the change is wrong.**   Many people resist change simply because they are unconvinced that management's proposed change will be effective. Anyone would find it hard to buy into a change that is doomed to fail. The belief that the change is wrong will be less of a problem if all company employees are involved in the change process. Under this category, we also must include resentment of the *method* used to make the change happen.

6. **Rebellion against the speed of the change.**   Change efforts often fail because the pace of change is inappropriate either to the nature of the situation or to the mood of the people. Without proper initiation or training, workers often engage in rebellion against the speed of the change. One typing pool supervisor removed all of the typewriters over a weekend, without warning the workers. When the workers were confronted on Monday morning with word processors they had never seen before, a rebellion took place. The other extreme is bringing about change too slowly. When the pace is so sluggish that workers sometimes question whether any real change is ever going to happen, negative attitudes often are the result.

---

[1] See: David A Nadir and Michael L Tushman, "Beyond the Charismatic Leader: Leadership and Organizational Change," *California Management Review* 32 (Winter 1990), pp. 77–97.

These reasons are listed so that you can more clearly understand what can frustrate you about a change when it takes place. With this self-knowledge, you can be more effective in dealing with your own stress and that of others when a change is in the works. Which reasons do you recognize in yourself and in others?

HOW TO COPE WHEN CHANGES HAPPEN

Several different types of organizational change require different strategies of coping. Let's look at two of the more likely kinds of change to affect you in the turn-of-the-century workplace.

Technological Changes

Technology will most certainly continue to grow and develop in the future, creating dramatic changes in the process. It's easy to see why many people become overwhelmed with **technological changes** and with the implications for their careers. In 19-century Europe, a worker named Ned Ludd was supposed to have smashed new machinery to protest the workplace changes it represented. Later, a Luddite movement was formed by workers who despised new technology and sought to destroy it when possible. Today's fast-changing technologies have produced a new group of "Luddites," workers—and sometimes managers—who wish that technological change would slow down.[2]

Are you a Luddite, or have you ever been tempted to think that way? If so, it should help you to know that the human element will continue far into the future to be the most important factor in the workplace. The fear that the worker is becoming increasingly less important in the workplace is simply not true over the long term. You, the human resource, will still be the most potent factor in the workplace regardless of the speed and complexity of technological change. Therefore, learn the new technologies, stay up to date, and don't become a Luddite.

---

[2] Paul Timm and Brent Peterson, *People at Work: Human Relations in Organizations* (Minneapolis: West Publishing, 1993), pp 422–23.

Downsizing

Retrenchment, or downsizing, is a company's reduction in the size of its workforce. It is likely to affect you at some time during your career. As an employee, you will have little or no control over downsizing. Often, employees in this kind of situation become victims of the rumor mill. You can take steps to help yourself, however.

1. Be thorough and careful in your investigation of the company's plans. When possible, ask management to reveal decisions as soon as they are reached.

2. If you are a likely target of downsizing, begin at once to look for another position. You can cancel your job-hunting plans much more readily than you can start them.

3. Don't allow the situation to hurt your self-esteem. Severely damaged self-esteem can paralyze you, and this is not the point in your life when you can afford to be paralyzed. Instead of worrying about the fairness of management choices, channel your energy into positive actions. Be the employee who stays one step ahead of management and who understands the realities of the job market. You are still the most important person in your own life.

Attitudes and Change

Whatever important changes take place in your company, you can take steps to make their effect less severe. All of them are aimed at a common objective: Keep a positive attitude toward change in the workplace.

1. Stress the positive. Remember the self-fulfilling prophecy; people who emphasize the negative often end up living with the consequences they feared most. This happens because they have somehow caused the events that they feared would take place.

2. Don't allow company gossip and other negative talk to get you down. Fearful co-workers will often make the problem worse by stressing negative possibilities. Enough real negatives are usually in the air during a time of change,

without the addition of rumormongers and prophets of doom.

3. ~~Don't waste your time blaming others.~~ Remember that you are ultimately the one person who cares the most about you and—more importantly—that you are the only one who can change your own life. Yes, others are often legitimately to blame for decisions that have affected you, and it doesn't take much thought to find the victims of your anger. However, you should make more constructive use of the energy consumed in blaming others to build positively for your future.

4. ~~Don't let fear control you.~~ Notice that we didn't say, "Don't be afraid." Fear is often inevitable in the realities of today's world. The point is not to allow fear to take over your planning, your judgment, or your decision making.

Change is a workplace factor we all have to face. The trick is to keep your attitude positive and avoid the pain and stress change can bring.

Key Terms

change	resentment toward the change agent	technological changes
perceptions of reality	belief that the change is wrong	Luddites
fear of the unknown	rebellion against the speed of the change	downsizing (retrenchment)
fear of loss		positive attitude toward change
change agent		

Review Questions

1. Discuss the relationship between workplace change and stress.
2. Why do many people resist change, even when they know it is unavoidable?
3. Think of changing situations where you have resisted change. What were your objections based upon?

4. Discuss the difference between dealing with downsizing and dealing with technological change. Give some examples.
5. Discuss the importance of *attitudes* in dealing with the change process.

Multiple Choice

1. Change is:
   a. Avoidable in any workplace if you are willing to take the right steps.
   b. Always a negative force in the workplace and should be avoided.
   c. Unavoidable in today's workplace and thus must be dealt with.
   d. Always caused by management.
2. Which of the following is *not* one of the major sources of opposition to change?
   a. Fear of the unknown.
   b. Individual perceptions of reality.
   c. Fear of loss.
   d. Fear of management.
3. Which of the following is one of the steps you can take to deal with downsizing?
   a. Refuse to allow the situation to hurt your self-esteem.
   b. Refuse to look for another job until you are sure that the downsizing will affect you directly.
   c. Make sure you don't ask management too many questions.
   d. Sit it out; it probably won't affect you anyway.
4. A Luddite is a person:
   a. Who is too lazy to work.
   b. Who hates new technology.
   c. Who can't get along with management.
   d. Who loves change.
5. What is the most important issue for you in your dealing with workplace change?
   a. Your salary
   b. Your boss
   c. Your co-workers
   d. Your attitude

The Video Store

Mark Wolford was a clerk in a large metropolitan video rental center. Happy with his job, Mark especially enjoyed talking about the latest movies and meeting new customers. One morning, his boss, Trent Locklear, met him at the front door.

Trent: Mark, there are going to be some big changes around here. First, we're going to convert to a new open-stack system to reduce the number of employees we need on each shift. I want you to learn this system thoroughly, and here's why. We're building a new store in the north end. It will have this system, too, and I want you to manage the store as soon as it's finished next month.

Mark: W-wow! [*stammering*]. I don't know what to say.

Trent: Well, you think it over and discuss it with your family. Let me know tomorrow.

Mark: Thanks, I will.

But for some reason, Mark felt as much fear as excitement. Yeah, I'm really going to have to think this over, Mark thought to himself.

1. How is Mark's promotion offer typical of workplace change? How is it different from most such changes?

2. If you were Trent Locklear, would you have handled these two simultaneous changes differently? If so, how?

3. Explain Mark Wolford's mixed feelings.

19

Are You Ever Caught in the Middle of a Conflict?

"Jaime, it's after 10 o'clock. If you're going to make the school bus in the morning, you need to get to bed."

"Aw, Mom, I'm 16 years old! Why are you treating me like a baby? I can get myself up in time for school!"

"Not if you're up all night playing those video games, you can't! Now go to bed! Honestly, I don't understand you teenagers! You don't listen and you don't do what you're told. You just turn everything your dad and I say into a big conflict!"

Conflicts are everywhere—at work, at home, in public, in private, between friends, between strangers. Wherever there are people, there are conflicts. Most definitions of conflict include the same ideas: A conflict must be *perceived* by the people involved in it, some *opposition* or *incompatibility* is involved, and some type of *interaction* is going on. We will define a **conflict** as a process that happens when someone believes that their property, ideas, or values are being damaged or threatened in some way.[1]

---

[1] Stephen P. Robbins, *Organizational Behavior: Concepts, Controversies, and Applications* (Englewood Cliffs, NJ: Prentice Hall, 1993), p. 445.

TYPES OF CONFLICT

We usually think of conflict only as being negative. But if conflict is approached in the right way, it can be helpful and constructive. One way to classify conflicts is to see them as either a **functional conflict** (constructive), or a **dysfunctional conflict** (destructive). For example, some lively discussion and disagreement in a work team (functional conflict) can bring out new ideas, but if this disagreement leads to arguments and insults (dysfunctional conflict), then any potential benefits are lost.

WHO IS INVOLVED IN THE CONFLICT?

Another way to classify a conflict is according to who is involved in it. There are four types of conflicts in this classification.

Inner Conflict

The **inner conflict** lies within a person. It is caused by contradictions in a person's inner loyalties, values, or priorities. For example, suppose your boss wants you to make a copy of a videotape that is protected by a copyright. You know it's illegal and unethical, but you want to protect your job. What do you do? Inner conflict also can happen when a person is pulled in opposite directions by two competing choices. For example, you may be really excited about being offered a promotion, but taking the promotion will mean moving to a new city, away from your friends and family.

Person-against-Person Conflict

This type of conflict involves people who are in a dispute because of personality differences, values differences, clashing loyalties, or anything else. In a **person-against-person conflict**, the focus is usually personal on both sides. In a college biology class, for example, two students may argue about creationism versus evolution. Both students may end up taking the conflict personally by feeling that they and their personal beliefs are under attack.

Within-Group Conflict

When individuals or subgroups within a larger group take sides
and clash with each other, a within-group conflict is occurring. For
example, suppose that a small company is having financial problems. Half of the staff wants to stay with the company and ride out
the problem, hoping things will improve. The other half wants to
quit unless the company can get its finances in order. People on
both sides of this conflict may get into ongoing arguments until the
conflict is resolved.

Person-against-Group Conflict

This type of conflict occurs when a member of a group breaks the
group's rules or norms. For example, a group of construction workers from the same company gets together to play poker every Friday night. When one of the regular players decides to stop joining
the group every week, the rest of the group makes fun of him and
treats him as an outsider at work. A person-against-group conflict
also can involve someone who opposes a group, but was never a
member of the group. For example, someone may oppose the National Rifle Association and work against or talk negatively about
the group because of things they have heard about it, without ever
having belonged to the group.

SOURCES OF CONFLICT

The four types of conflict above describe who is involved in conflicts, but don't tell us how conflicts start. Disagreements are all different. They start at different points over different issues. Four common types of these different sources of conflicts are described
below.

Content Conflict

A disagreement that focuses on the meaning of a statement or a
concept is called a content conflict. Whether an idea is right or
wrong usually focuses on one of two factors: existence or meaning.
Two people who are arguing about whether Bigfoot is real are arguing about existence. If the same two people are arguing about

whether making coffee is part of their job, they are arguing about meaning.

Conflicts about existence.   Conflicts about existence can be settled if verification is possible. Many people believe that Bigfoot exists, but they have not been able to prove it. Even more difficult is proving that Bigfoot—or UFOs, or conspiracies about President Kennedy's assassination, or the Loch Ness monster, or even God—does *not* exist. That's why conflicts over existence are not settled. When proof is available, people can use that proof to settle the conflict.

Conflicts about meaning.   Conflicts about meaning can be settled if the people involved can trace the conflict back to the original ambiguous wording and agree on an interpretation.

Values Conflict

Conflicts about values usually go very deep. For example, an atheist and a fundamentalist Christian will probably not agree on how life began, no matter how hard they try. In the workplace, managers may have serious disagreements about management practices. The values conflict has its roots in basic values and beliefs about people and how they should be treated. Values conflicts can be solved by listening carefully and communicating your values to the other person. This allows a sense of trust and mutual respect for others to develop. Values conflicts also can be avoided by having a greater tolerance for other people's values.

Negotiation-of-Selves Conflict

A negotiation-of-selves conflict can happen when our self-perception is distorted and differences arise over self-definition. Employees probably see themselves differently than management sees them, children see themselves differently than their parents see them, and so on.

We are constantly involved in the process of defining ourselves—unnoticed and unspoken—to others and reacting to the way others see us. For example, a customer is trying to return a set of china to a store without a receipt. The customer is not likely to say, "I'm acting humble and apologetic so that you will feel sorry for me and give me my money back." The clerk, at the same time, is not likely to say, "I'm acting snooty and rude to you because I feel superior to you, and I have the keys to the cash register, and I want you to suck up to me." Nonverbal cues in situations such as these are hard to interpret because both sides are involved in playing a role and negotiation of selves.

Institutional Conflict

A conflict that is built into the structure of an organization is called an **institutional conflict.** This conflict happens when groups in an organization look at decisions as if they involve a gain for one person or group at the expense of others. For example, groups frequently see organization budget decisions as competing for limited pieces of a funding pie. No group is completely happy with the outcome.

Some organizations also have unclear policies or rules about who will do what type of work or what job assignments. This causes conflict among people in the organization about who is responsible for what tasks. In the end, the task may not get done or it may be late, and there will be hard feelings all around.

ANALYZING CONFLICTS

Anyone who wants to resolve a conflict should start by taking a close look—an analysis—at what is really happening. When strong emotions are involved, we are tempted to jump to conclusions before we have examined the interests of both sides or our own interests. To figure out what is really happening, ask yourself the following questions about the conflict.

1. **Who is involved?**   How many people are involved in the conflict? How well do they understand the basic issues? Are any of these people constantly in conflict, or is this an unusual situation? By knowing these details, a leader can do a better job of planning how to resolve the conflict so that everyone's interests are met.

2. **What is at stake?**   Do all or both sides in the conflict agree about what is really at stake? If duties or responsibilities are at stake, does everyone agree on exactly what those issues are? If money is involved, is everyone talking about the same amount?

Does the conflict involve assigning blame for misconduct, or could the issue be one of defining proper conduct for the future? Without this step, the entire issue may become blurred.

3. How important is time? Does this conflict have to be settled right away to meet everyone's best interests? Does one side or the other benefit from stalling? A conflict manager or leader should consider the time factor. Allowing some time to pass could cool tempers, but it also could aggravate the issue.

4. How does this issue tie in with other issues? Is this conflict related to other disputes between the same people or groups? Will working relationships be affected by the outcome?

After you answer these questions, you can decide whether the issue is worth resolving. If you decide that it is, the conflict can be resolved by following the steps in Chapter 20.

Key Terms

conflict

functional conflict

dysfunctional conflict

inner conflict

person-against-person conflict

within-group conflict

person-against-group conflict

content conflict

values conflict

negotiation-of-selves conflict

institutional conflict

Review Questions

1. You have been asked to analyze a conflict between two co-workers over who was supposed to finish a report for Hitchcock Manufacturing Company. What steps would you take in analyzing this conflict?

2. How would you classify the conflict in the example above; that is, who is involved? To which category of sources does it belong?

3. What is the difference between a functional conflict and a dysfunctional conflict? Can you turn a dysfunctional conflict into a functional conflict? If so, how?

4. Think of situations in which you were involved in a within-group conflict and in a person-against-group conflict. How were these situations different?
5. Has someone close to you ever put you in a situation where you felt inner conflict? If so, describe this situation. Have you ever done this to anyone else, even unintentionally?

Multiple Choice

1. When analyzing a conflict, an important question to ask is:
   a. What time is it now?
   b. What is at stake?
   c. Who can be hired to resolve it?
   d. How is this issue different from other issues?
2. When two friends argue about which political party is better for this country, what type of conflict is gong on?
   a. Values
   b. Content
   c. Context
   d. Negotiation-of-selves
3. Two people having a heated discussion of whether vampires and werewolves are real, are having a conflict about:
   a. Values
   b. Existence
   c. Meaning
   d. Negotiation-of-selves
4. Two children are discussing whether the Tooth Fairy is real and how they should go about finding out. This conflict is:
   a. Institutionalized
   b. Dysfunctional
   c. Functional
   d. None of the above
5. When a person breaks a group's rules or norms, what type of conflict can occur?
   a. Person-against-group
   b. Person-against-person
   c. Intragroup
   d. Intergroup

Which Way Is West?

The air was thick with tension in the sales office of Nationwide Pharmaceuticals. The new sales staff had just come into town for their first full group meeting, and the three newest representatives were involved in a heated conflict over whose territory included what areas. All three believed that their territory had been trampled on and customers stolen by the other two.

Lance: Everyone knows that when you say "Western states," that means the states on the West Coast *only!* Washington, Oregon, and California! You should have stayed out of my area!

Chloe: That's ridiculous! "Western states" means everything west of the Mississippi! They're *all* my states!

Vittorio: You're both crazy! The "Western states" include the western half of the United States, plus Alaska and Hawaii! You stole my best clients!

1. Is this a conflict over negotiation-of-selves, values, or content? Why? Is there an easy way to resolve this conflict?

2. Analyze this conflict: Who is involved? (Is anyone involved outside of the three sales people above?) How important is time? (In any sales setting, is time important?) What is at stake? From the information above, can you tell if this issue is linked to other issues?

3. Is this a functional conflict or a dysfunctional conflict? Why? Can it change (to functional from dysfunctional, or dysfunctional to functional)?

20

You Can Be a Negotiator

Mike Curry and Tim Burns were arguing one morning in the carpentry shop where they work. Things were tense at work because new management had taken over the month before. The new system of keeping tools locked up in a central toolbox meant that everyone had to find Wes Ward, the foreman, when they needed something. Because everyone's tools were kept together, workers often grabbed someone else's tools whenever they were in a hurry. That's what caused Mike and Tim's argument. Tim had wasted an hour looking for his nail gun before finding it in Mike's area under a cabinet drawer. Both of them marched over to see Wes.

"Wes," said Mike, "this tool situation is getting way out of hand."

"You'd better figure this out pretty quickly, Wes," said Tim, "or I quit!"

Wes was as tired of the tool storage situation as his workers. "Just get back to work!" he said in an annoyed tone. "I don't care whose tools were where! If you don't like the new rules, then find a new job!"

In Chapter 19, we talked about conflicts and deciding which issues are worth resolving. If you've decided that an issue is worth being resolved, this chapter can help you to do that.

STRATEGIES TO RESOLVE CONFLICTS

Conflicts can be resolved in three ways: win-lose, lose-lose, and win-win. The first two strategies are not likely to solve the problem very well. They will produce negative outcomes and result in people taking sides. They are Band-Aid solutions that leave the real problem ready to surface again later. Sometimes, however, time limits and an unwillingness to work toward a win-win solution might cause you to use a lose-lose or win-lose strategy.

Win-Lose

In the win-lose strategy, one side will win at the other side's expense.[1] It is a quick-fix solution that sometimes must be chosen when a win-win approach can't be used. One type of win-lose approach is the democratic vote. Democracy seems like a great approach to resolving conflicts, but it leaves a minority of unhappy people without any say in what happens. This minority may bring the problem back later, possibly in another form.

Another win-lose strategy is the arbitrary approach, in which the person in charge states which side is right and which is wrong, or which will win and which will lose. When the arbitrary approach is used, losers tend to have hard feelings against the winning side and the leader. This type of solution is usually short term only, and problems causing the conflicts won't end.

Lose-Lose

In the lose-lose strategy, everybody gives something up. The main approach in lose-lose is compromise—compromise in the sense that nobody gets what they want, everyone gains a little, and both sides can live with the decision. Like win-lose, this strategy also does not solve the underlying cause of the conflict. Unlike win-lose, there are unhappy people on both sides of the issue in the lose-lose strategy. The arbitrator who determines the outcome in the lose-lose strategy pays little attention to the history of the conflict, so the solutions again are usually short term.[2]

---

[1] Edward Glassman, "Selling Your Ideas to Management," *Supervisory Management*, Oct. 1991, p. 9.

[2] Barry L. Reece and Rhonda Brandt, *Effective Human Relations in Organizations* (Boston: Houghton Mifflin, 1993), pp. 356–58.

Win-Win

In a **win-win** strategy, both sides feel they came out on top. It might seem impossible that both sides could win, but because most conflicts start from several sources and reasons, they are complex enough so that both sides can win something. People usually place different priorities on their reasons for getting into a conflict. Usually, they will be satisfied with small victories that are less than the entire package of results they are fighting for. The key to success in a win-win strategy is to satisfy as many of the needs as possible on both sides of the conflict.

NEGOTIATING WIN-WIN SOLUTIONS

The **conflict manager** or leader should try to find the underlying reasons, the interests, and the needs on each side of the conflict. Once these are figured out, the conflict manager can get each side to list its needs in order of importance. The rest of the negotiation process is a series of **concessions,** in which each side gives up on one issue in order to gain on another. At this point in the process, creativity is very important. A creative negotiator can think of bargaining moves that would not occur to someone less creative. **Concession bargaining** is the process of getting each side in a conflict to make concessions willingly. Union bargaining teams often use this technique. This process isn't as easy as it sounds. The conflict manager must take the group through a series of steps, following some important guidelines, before the win-win method can work. Here are six steps to follow in a successful win-win strategy.

1. **Control emotions.** If emotions are strong on one side or both sides, an arbitrator will have to put most of the creative effort into clearing the air and calming people down. Leaders should be careful that they don't get their own emotions involved on either side. A good beginning might be:

> *Look, I can see that you're angry. But if we're going to resolve this, we need to put that anger aside and work on alternatives. Are you willing to try?*

It is crucial that people on both sides put their emotions aside and work on problems instead of getting stuck in blaming each other. Anger itself can become another source of conflict when one person's anger feeds the anger of the other. Anger must be expressed, but it will block communication when expressed too strongly. If nothing else gets done, at least the leader can get both sides to explain why they are angry. The focus can then become the reasons for feelings, rather than the feelings alone.

2. **Agree on ground rules.** Once the anger is dealt with, the conflict manager can set ground rules. These rules are meant to keep the process running smoothly, not to force either side to conform. Some of the basic rules could include:

Agree to listen carefully, without interrupting.

Agree to control anger, even if someone disagrees with you.

Agree to treat each other with the same respect you would like to receive.

Agree on the amount of time to spend trying to solve the problem.

Agreeing to put yourself in the place of the other.

Both sides should suggest rules at the time ground rules are being set. The earlier in the process rules are set, the better. Once set, ground rules can be used later as calming and disciplinary tools if the discussion threatens to get out of hand. By reminding each side of the rules they had agreed upon, the leader has a better chance of keeping control.

3. **Make sure all positions are clear.** Now it is time to get all the issues, facts, and opinions out on the table. When both sides have seen the problems from the other's perspective, they can move toward an understanding that makes them both feel like winners. While still pushing for whatever they want most, both sides will also be listening to the needs of the other side. It is important that the conflict manager maintain his or her objectivity and avoid making value judgments. The conflict manager should allow both sides equal time for self-expression and prevent any one side from dominating the discussion.

4. **Explore several needs and issues.** The conflict manager should begin this phase by allowing both sides to explain why they chose their positions instead of the other position. Then find multiple interests in the issue. Look for the issues and interests that both sides share.

5. **Develop alternative plans.** List several possible alternatives,

based on the needs and issues you uncovered. Keep track of these in order to examine them carefully later. This can be like a brainstorming session. Don't allow either side to make value judgments or biased comments. The goal is a large number of ideas rather than a few good ones.

6. **Choose win-win solutions.**   Explain carefully what a win-win solution is: one that gives something of value to both sides. Then go through each alternative, asking how it can be seen as a win-win solution. A list of solutions that both sides can agree upon will usually evolve. If that doesn't happen, the conflict manager has to make the decisions alone, asking for compliance with the solutions he or she accepts.

For these six steps to work, several requirements have to be met. First, everyone involved in the conflict must be willing to go through the steps. They must get rid of their fight-to-win attitudes. Second, everyone involved has to be willing to take the time to complete the entire process. Win-win strategies are sometimes abandoned because they take too long. Third, the conflict manager must be flexible, sensitive, patient, and calm under fire.

STYLES OF CONFLICT MANAGEMENT

Everyone has his or her style of handling conflicts. Usually these styles fit into one of five common styles. The style you use will have a big impact on the outcome of a conflict, making it more positive or negative. See whether one of these styles fits with yours.

Competitor

People who follow the competitor style of conflict management actively try to get their own way. They usually use a win-lose approach, especially if they are actively involved in the conflict. Neutral leaders who are competitors may use a lose-lose style. Teamwork is not a goal. Competitors don't like the disruption of a conflict, so they work quickly and energetically to get rid of it. Competitors rarely use a win-win strategy.

Avoider

Those who follow the avoider style try to keep away from the conflict or to remain neutral. They may say positive things about the conflict situation when asked about it or they may pretend that nothing has happened. But the avoider often feels a lot of internal stress while the conflict is going on.

Compromiser

If you follow the compromiser style of conflict resolution, you will try to work out a solution where both sides give up a little to get some of what they want. Compromisers use their skills to find alternatives. They tend to see an agreement as more important than the issue itself. Compromisers usually don't feel rushed to find a solution as competitors do, but they may settle for a lose-lose compromise. Compromisers can find a win-win solution if they follow the steps in that process.

Accommodator

People who adopt the accommodator style try to work out a solution in which people give up a little of what they want. Accommodators might have a "don't worry, be happy" attitude toward people on both sides. They try to avoid conflict by urging people to think positively. They tell people to "count your blessings" or "look on the bright side." Keeping the manager happy is also a top priority for accommodators.

Collaborator

Collaborators try to work with others—collaborating—to achieve a solution that satisfies both sides. They are most likely to bring about a win-win solution. The collaborator style is necessary for a win-win solution, but it requires more skills than other styles. This explains why many conflict managers often fall back upon one of the simpler styles.

QUALITIES OF AN EFFECTIVE CONFLICT RESOLUTION METHOD

Successful conflict resolution methods have several things in common. All successful methods:

1. **Make interests clear.** This is done by encouraging both sides to examine the real best interests of their positions, by helping to ex-

plore what interests they have in common, and by communicating each side's interests to the other side without letting one side take advantage of the other.

2. **Build a good working relationship.** This is done by giving both sides a chance to deal with their differences, by encouraging a relationship that both sides would have wanted if it weren't for the dispute, and by making it easier for both sides to deal with each other the next time.

3. **Generate good opinions.** This is done by encouraging both sides to brainstorm different options before choosing one and by encouraging both sides to come up with creative, helpful solutions.

4. **View as legitimate by both sides.** This is done by causing one side not to give up more than the other, by being seen as not going against the public interest, and by letting both sides feel that the solution will be fair.

5. **Improve communication.** This is done by encouraging both sides to ask questions, by helping both sides understand the different perceptions of the situation, and by helping to establish two-way communication between people making the decisions.

6. **Lead to wise commitments.** This is done by enabling both sides to develop commitments that are realistic, useful, and most likely to prevent future conflicts; and by putting both sides in positions where they can seek out legal recourse if the agreement breaks down or is not honored.

WORK TOGETHER WITH OTHERS

In collaborating with others, conflict resolution is a problem-solving process that includes four phases:

1. **Identify the problem.** Make sure you are dealing with the real issue, not some other problem. Otherwise, even an apparently win-win solution will really be dealing with symptoms instead of problems.

2. **Develop a solution.** A group can take this step in many different ways, from group discussions to written questionnaires. For this phase to work, all people directly affected by the conflict should be included.

3. **Identify an action plan.** Get an agreement from both sides to follow the action plan.

4. **Put the action plan to work.**   Then follow up on the results. The follow-up is important in preventing future harmful conflicts.

STOP CONFLICTS BEFORE THEY START

The best way to handle any negative conflict is to prevent it from happening. Of course, no workplace or organization is ever completely without conflicts, but managers and employees can take steps to prevent many conflicts, and to soften the impact of those that do happen. Here are some suggestions on how to do this.

1. **Turn the people around you into winners.**   People who feel like winners are less likely to start conflicts. Self-esteem is a key to conflict management. Whatever you can do as a leader or employee to boost the self-esteem of others is likely to prevent conflict. Also, allow others to be successful at the work they are doing, whenever possible, to help boost their self-esteem.

2. **Work together on common goals.** When an organization works toward common goals, there is little room for conflict. But many times those goals are not clear and workers stumble around in a fog, working more toward their own goals than on the purposes of the group as a whole. If you are a manager, help your staff recognize that the common goals they share are more important than personal status. If you are a group member, ask questions so that you are clear about the common goals.

3. **Communicate.**   Listen carefully for hints that people are not happy. When you need to say something, find the right time and place to say it, then say it in a clear and tactful way.

 ## Key Terms

win-lose	conflict manager	avoider style
democratic vote	concessions	compromiser style
arbitrary approach	concession	accommodator
lose-lose	bargaining	style
compromise	ground rules	collaborating
arbitrator	objectivity	collaborator style
win-win	competitor style	

Review Questions

1. What are the steps needed to reach a win-win outcome? What type of conflict management style is most likely to achieve a win-win outcome?
2. What suggestions can be used to set ground rules in conflict management? Would these suggestions work for resolving conflicts in your personal life? Explain.
3. Which of the common styles of conflict manager most fits your style? Why? Is there a style that might work better for you?
4. What is the difference between accommodating, collaborating, and compromising? Which style works best in reaching a win-win solution?
5. In the United States, we believe in the value of the democratic process as a government style. But in this chapter, you saw some of the problems with this process as a way to resolve conflicts. How do you explain this apparent contradiction?

Multiple Choice

1. Jessie hates confrontation and stays away from it whenever possible. Which style of conflict management would be best for her?
   a. Accommodator
   b. Avoider
   c. Collaborator
   d. Compromiser
2. Suggestions for stopping conflicts before they start include all of the following *except:*
   a. Turning people around you into winners.
   b. Working together on common goals.
   c. Communicating better.
   d. Setting up healthy competition between workers.
3. A lose-lose strategy is most likely to come from which style of conflict management?
   a. Compromiser
   b. Avoider
   c. Collaborator
   d. Accommodator

4. Which of the following steps should be taken *first* in negotiating a win-win solution?

   a. Agree on ground rules.

   b. Make all positions clear.

   c. Set ground rules.

   d. Get emotions under control.

5. A successful conflict resolution method includes such qualities as:

   a. Being seen by one of the sides as legitimate.

   b. Reducing communication between the two sides.

   c. Building a good working relationship on both sides.

   d. Hiding each side's interests from the other side.

Case 20-1

Win-Winning at Work

Enrique Paradiso was the head of the public relations department at a large firm. His two staff writers, Mary Wagner and Linda Kelly, got along great most of the time. But on this particular morning, things were not going well. Mary and Linda both thought that Enrique had assigned the other writer to finish the company newsletter, which was scheduled to go out today, so neither one had done it.

Enrique was having a hard time remembering the steps to a win-win solution while both writers were talking to him at the same time. I've got to think, let's see, he thought to himself. I know the first thing to do is to calm everybody down. But then what?

   1. What are the rest of the steps that Enrique is forgetting?

   2. How can Enrique, Mary, and Linda collaborate to resolve this conflict?

   3. What can Enrique do now to stop a conflict before it starts the next time?

21

How to Become the Person the Customer Asks For

"Where's that nice young lady who waited on me last time I was here?" asked an elderly woman as she approached the cosmetics counter. "What am I, chopped liver?" Betsy thought to herself. Bassima, the clerk the lady described, was out on break. "I'd be glad to help," Betsy replied in a kind voice. "No, that's fine; I'll be back in 15 minutes," was the answer. Why do so many customers ask for Bassima? Betsy asked herself. She's only been in this country for a few years and speaks broken English, she's overweight, and she's only been at this job for a year. This is my third year here. Argh! Betsy became increasingly upset as she reflected. Finally, she calmed down. I know what I'm going to do, she told herself. I'm going to start watching Bassima like a hawk to see if I can figure out what makes the customers so crazy over her.

Have you ever felt like Betsy? If you have, you know how tempting it is to be jealous and to rationalize that the issue is one of personal charm and magnetism—nothing you could duplicate. Of course, outstanding personality and appearance are often involved, but most of the important qualities that make you sought after by customers and clients involve *skills that can be taught*.

In a larger sense, nearly everyone with whom you come in contact at work is a customer. If you are a manager, your employees are customers. Although this chapter focuses on the traditional definition of a customer, many of the issues raised also will apply to internal, external, and would-be customers.

UNDERSTANDING THE NEEDS OF THE CUSTOMER

What do customers want when they enter your place of business? If you look at each situation carefully, you will notice that they want one of two things—and often both: good feelings and solutions to problems.[1] Virtually everything that a customer wants from you and your business will fall into one of those categories. For example:

- You don't sell clothes. You're selling a sharp appearance, style, attractiveness, and warmth.
- You don't sell car washes. You sell pride in owning a sparkling clean automobile and a feeling of importance.
- You don't sell airline tickets. You sell convenience, good treatment, and safety.
- You don't sell toys. You sell happy moments for children.

In a sense, you don't sell things or services at all. You sell good feelings and solutions to problems. Apparently, Bassima has learned how to use this principle successfully. Every moment you are on the job, think about feelings and solutions. Make those two goals the most important activities you perform. If you do, your relations with customers will automatically improve.[2]

In a sense, every customer has a problem. The problem might be simply that the customer doesn't yet have the goods or services that your company provides. Or perhaps the problem is dissatisfaction with some part of your operation. Learn to focus on the problem. Ask what can I do that will solve the problem as the customer sees it? Your treatment of customers and their real needs is the key to your success in any business. See the various needs in the box.

---

[1] Michael LeBoeuf, *How to Win Customers and Keep Them for Life* (New York: Putnam, 1987), pp. 38–40.
[2] Ibid., p. 39.

Basic Human Needs in Customers

- The need to be accepted by others.
- The need to feel comfortable.
- The need to feel appreciated.
- The need to be recognized by name or face.
- The need to be treated with respect.
- The need to be welcomed and acknowledged.
- The need to be listened to.
- The need to be treated with fairness.
- The need to be treated as an individual instead of as a member of a group.

TWO SIMPLE PRINCIPLES OF CUSTOMER SERVICE

The two principles that can make all of the difference in succeeding with customers are deceptively simple:

1. Find out what the customer needs.
2. Do what is necessary to satisfy that need.

Nothing could be easier, yet so many people who deal with customers miss these two simple principles. The first principle of customer service skills involves listening and asking questions. Don't jump to the conclusion that you know what the customer needs. Remember that the real needs are problem solutions and good feelings. If you aren't getting information that takes care of those two categories, keep asking questions until you find it. The second principle involves making sure that you have the solution and that it is the best one for the customer.

What if the wants of the customer don't seem to fit with what your company provides? What if the customer doesn't even want to buy anything? Take a second look. Let's say you work for a restaurant as a cashier. Someone comes in from the street and asks for change for a $20 bill. Is this person a customer? The answer is a definite yes. Your best procedure would be to treat that person with the same courtesy that you would extend to a customer who just finished a meal and was paying for it. The change-getter's opinion of your establishment might bring her in again, and she has family and friends who are potential customers.

Customers and self-esteem. Customers are people like anyone else. Like the rest of us, self-esteem is important to them. Anything you do to damage customer self-esteem will work against your business. Happily, the opposite is also true. Anything you can do to cause your customers to feel better about themselves—even the smallest actions you take—will improve your chances for repeat business. We will cover this topic more fully in Chapter 23.

BONDING WITH THE CUSTOMER

If you want to be the person customers ask for, you need to establish a bond with your customers. This most important practice of **bonding with the customer** also is known in business as **relationship selling.** Once you have established a meaningful relationship with a customer, trust and confidence are greatly enhanced, and repeat business is much more likely.

1. Understand the customer's real needs. As mentioned, careful *listening* to the customer can make up for a great number of deficiencies in a company. Think about your relationship with someone who is trying to sell a product or service to you. Wouldn't you rather deal with someone who is tuned into your needs, desires and whims?

2. If your customer is another business, learn about that business. Customers will be more likely to bond with you if you show a genuine understanding of their business and what that business means to them personally and professionally. You can read annual reports, trade journals, newspaper and magazine articles to acquaint yourself with their business.

3. Provide exceptional service. Exceptional service provides the strongest bond of all. **Exceptional service** means providing the best service you possibly can. If you are an employee, providing exceptional service isn't always completely up to you. Even as a manager, you might not have control over the quality of service that you would like to have. But you can be creative; usually it is possible to innovate in your own niche.

4. Really care.   Pretending isn't enough; customers can usually see right through it. Be the person who cultivates a genuine caring for your customers as human beings. There is no substitute for genuine caring. Part of caring is making sure the customer doesn't walk out with negative feelings. Some people who work in or run businesses make the incorrect assumption that if anything is wrong, the customer will say so. But, most customers are too "nice" to let their true negative feelings show. See the box about the "nice" customer. The nice customers don't complain when a problem arises, but neither do they come back for repeat business nor do they recommend your product or services to anyone.

The Nice Customer

I'm a nice customer. You all know me. I'm the one who never complains, no matter what kind of service I get.

I'll go into a restaurant and sit quietly while the waiters and waitresses gossip and never bother to ask if anyone has taken my order. Sometimes a party that came in after I did gets my order, but I don't complain. I just wait.

And when I go to a store to buy something, I don't throw my weight around. I try to be thoughtful of the other person. If a snooty salesperson gets upset because I want to look at several things before making up my mind, I'm just as polite as can be. I don't believe rudeness in return is the answer.

The other day I stopped at a full-service gas station and waited for almost five minutes before the attendant took care of me. And when he did, he spilled gas and wiped the windshield with an oily rag. But did I complain about the service? Of course not.

I never kick. I never nag. I never criticize. And I wouldn't dream of making a scene, as I've seen some people do in public places. I think that's uncalled for. No, I'm the nice customer. And I'll tell you who else I am.

I'm the customer who never comes back!

—Author unknown
(but nice)

GOING THE EXTRA MILE

A well-known owner of a restaurant chain in the Pacific Northwest tells the story of a new waiter he hired years ago. A longtime customer asked the new waiter why the customary pickle wasn't included in his hamburger. The new waiter retorted, "A pickle will cost you an extra dime." When the owner heard the story, he coined a phrase which he now often uses when he speaks in public: "Give them the pickle!"

"Giving the customer the pickle" is simply good business. How do you feel when you ask for extra help at a retail store only to hear the salesclerk say, "Sorry, I'm too busy right now"? Is it likely that you will come back to that store? Also, won't you be likely to tell your friends and family about the incident? By not giving the little "extra" to you, the store has probably lost at least a dozen future purchases. Here are some examples of "**going the extra mile**":[3]

Ticket agent:	Would you like a window seat, or would you prefer to be on the aisle?
Salesperson:	I'll see to it personally that this is installed by tomorrow.
Bank clerk:	Take this new checkbook cover. Yours looks a little tired.
Grocery clerk:	That's a big load. Let me help you carry out those groceries.
Receptionist:	This is a big, confusing building. Let me draw you a little map.
Loan officer:	I can't tell you now, but I'll call you by 10:00 AM tomorrow.

How many of the above examples would really cost the company any significant money? The payback in customer relations is well worth the trifling cost. Courtesy, going the extra distance, always pays for itself.

Using the hints in this chapter, you can become the employee or manager whom customers ask for. You will find that the resulting position will become a very powerful one for you. If you are adding

---

[3] These examples are based on William B. Martin, *Quality Customer Service: The Art of Treating Customers as Guests* (Los Altos, CA: Crisp Publications, 1987), p. 63.

to business because of customer approval, your odds for security and advancement at work will increase. You also will be a happier person with a lower stress level.

Key Terms

feelings and solutions

two simple principles

customer service skills

customer self-esteem

bonding with the customer

relationship selling

exceptional service

the "nice" customer

"going the extra mile"

Review Questions

1. Explain the following: Customers really want only feelings and solutions rather than products and services.
2. What are the two simple principles of customer service? What importance does listening play in the use of those principles?
3. Explain the importance of customer bonding. How does one go about establishing this bond?
4. What is meant by "going the extra mile"? Provide an example.
5. Why is an understanding of the "nice customer" of great importance in improving customer service?

Multiple Choice

1. The skills that one needs to learn for success at customer relations:
   a. Are difficult to learn.
   b. Are mostly inborn qualities such as good looks and personality.
   c. Are skills that can be learned.
   d. Usually do little good in the long run.
2. What two things do most customers really want when they enter a place of business?
   a. Goods and services.
   b. Good feelings and solutions to problems.

   c. Attention and obedience.
   d. Goals and promises.
3. What are the two simple principles of customer service?
   a. Customer self-esteem and sales ability.
   b. Product sales and service sales.
   c. Courtesy and stamina.
   d. Discover the customer's needs and fulfill them.
4. What should you do if someone who is not a customer comes
   to your retail business and asks for change for a $10 bill?
   a. Very politely tell them that you can't make change for
      noncustomers.
   b. Very politely tell them that you'll do it this once, but not to
      ask for the favor a second time.
   c. Treat the person the same as if he or she were a paying
      customer.
   d. Ask them to speak to your manager.
5. Which of the following is *not* one of the guidelines for
   bonding with the customer?
   a. Understanding the customer's real needs.
   b. Providing excellent service.
   c. Asking plenty of questions.
   d. Showing that you really care.

**Case
21–1**

The New Car

Alice Lin was taking some time off work to fulfill her lifelong dream of buying a brand-new car. She had done some checking. Not only had she spent
weeks poring over brochures from various automakers, but also she had
read articles in Consumer Reports on all of the cars in her price range. At
the first dealership, she was snubbed by three salespeople before she found
one who took her seriously. The second try was about the same. By the
time she had approached the third car lot, she had lost some of her initial
enthusiasm.

But that was where she found the car of her dreams. After she test-
drove the car, the salesman, Bob, took her into his office and asked her to
make an offer. "Any offer; just whatever you think is reasonable," he said.

Alice had vacationed in Mexico a few times and was used to the principle of bargaining. She started with a very low price—about $3,000 below the price on the sticker. "Well, I'll see what I can do," Bob replied. "I'll have to ask the boss; I hope he's in a good mood."

Twenty minutes later, Alice walked to the back of the showroom to the candy machine. She heard a familiar voice ask someone, "Well, d'ya think I've stalled this one long enough?" It was now clear that Bob had not discussed this offer with his boss. Alice asked one of customer service people the whereabouts of the sales manager; "He's gone for the day" was the reply.

Quickly, Alice scurried back to Bob's office. When Bob walked in a minute later, he said without pausing, "Well, I'm sorry. The boss just won't go for your offer, but let's see if we can work out a deal that will be almost as good." Bob was startled when Alice answered, "I refuse to play any more of your silly, time-wasting games!" and walked out.

1. What procedures and attitudes covered in this chapter could have helped Bob make the sale to Alice?

2. The Saturn division of General Motors is one of several automobile companies that is trying to change the traditional methods of selling cars in this country. As a potential customer, what advice would you give them?

3. What suggestions would you give car dealers who use Bob's tactics?

22

How to Tell People News They Don't Want to Hear

Lindy was in line at a crowded membership department store with her husband, Carl, one busy Saturday morning. She had written her check out, except for the amount, while the clerk rang up the sale.

Clerk: Can I see your membership card? [*Carl shows her his card.*]

Clerk: This isn't your card, [*to Lindy, ignoring Carl*]

Lindy: No, it's my husband's card. I couldn't find mine. But we have the same membership number, it's a joint account.

Clerk: [*Annoyed*] I don't care, either *you* bring your card in, or *he* shows his card *and* writes the check!

Lindy: But it's the same account! And I've already written out the . . ."

Clerk: [*Angrily*] I *told* you what you have to do! Now move out of line, you're keeping people waiting! Next customer, please!

Lindy: That does it! [*to Carl*] I've had bad experiences here before, and this is the last straw. They obviously don't care about keeping customers. We're never shopping here again.

One of the most delicate tasks we have in dealing with other people is to give them bad news, especially when they are expecting good news. In the workplace, this can happen in many different situations—for example, when an employee has to turn down a customer's request for a refund or a bank loan; when a manager has to discipline, demote, or fire an employee; or when an instructor has to give a student a low or failing grade. No matter how often we have to deliver bad news, it never gets any easier for many of us. But by developing sound **bad news skills,** we can make the job less unpleasant.

STEPS IN DELIVERING BAD NEWS

Developing bad news skills takes some time, but it is not difficult if you use four suggested steps. These skills will make the delivery of bad news to customers easier on you and on them. If you are not delivering service to customers, substitute the appropriate term (such as "family member," "co-worker," "club member," "student," and so on) for the word "customer" in honing your bad news skills.

1. Be polite.   Use a polite tone of voice. Make it a point to listen to yourself as someone else would hear you. For most of us, the tone of voice we use is mostly unconscious, unless we specifically take notice of it. Pay attention to other nonverbal signals too, such as your facial expression and body posture. If your voice sounds sincere but you are looking annoyed and your body posture says that you're feeling impatient, then you may come off sounding sarcastic.

2. Don't overapologize.   Don't spend too much time on apologies. They may be necessary—and most customers will want to hear them—but most of us would rather understand the reasons for the bad news and know that some action is being taken to resolve whatever has gone wrong.

3. Explain the "whys".   Deal with *why* the problem exists. If you don't know, find out. If you are responsible for delivering the bad news, then you are also responsible for explaining why it is necessary. If it is impossible to figure out why the problem happened, go to step 4.

4. **Talk about solutions.**   Talk about what can be done to solve the problem. This should include any suggestions for alternative solutions from which the customer can choose, if that is possible. When only one option is available, explain to the customer why that action is best or the only option. Sell the customer on that idea.

Most customers do not like to hear, "Because it's company policy," as a reason for problems that have happened or why there are no alternative solutions. The "company policy" reason is often seen as an excuse. Even when it's true, it sounds weak. If you work for a manager who tells you that you must use that line, at least find out the reasoning behind the policy, so that you can explain it clearly and completely to the customer.

ENCOURAGING COMPLAINTS FROM CUSTOMERS IN A WORKPLACE SETTING

Why would we want to *encourage* complaints from customers? Because sometimes that's the *only* way we hear about a problem. Problems happen all the time. When we talk about a customer–company service situation, in a sense every customer who walks in the door has some kind of problem. **Customer complaints** may be about something simple—that they haven't been served yet or they haven't yet bought the wonderful product you are selling—or it may be more complex, such as the customer is unhappy with your service or product. Learn to focus on the problem. Ask yourself, What can I do to solve the problem as this person sees it?

Learning to anticipate problems or figure them out before they've happened means that you don't have to rely on the lack of customers to tell you that something is wrong. One of the easiest, but most unpleasant, ways to learn that there is a problem is by hearing from the angry, screaming customer. In a later chapter we'll talk about how to deal with these kind of people. But they are really in the minority. It is much more common to have the "nice" customers (see Chapter 21). These customers would actually be better for your business if they weren't so nice.

Customer report cards.   Many companies today realize that customer complaints are necessary, and that they should be encouraged in every way possible. This is why many restaurants, stores, and businesses offer a **customer report card**, which allows us to let the business know how they're doing in a nonthreatening, nonconfrontational way. Some restaurants and manufacturers even offer rewards for complaining by giving free products to people who have complained about bad service or products.

DEVELOPING A NEW ATTITUDE

If you're in a position to do so, try to influence everyone in your company to think positively about customers who complain. Without them, you have only a vague idea of what is wrong. Instead of calling them "complainers," how about a less negative name such as consultants, critics, or company allies?

A way to start encouraging customer complaints is to start rethinking what they are. They are opportunities to improve service when the company might not have thought there was a need for it. It is also necessary to rethink what complaints are not. They are not meant as personal attacks or signals that the relationship between the customer and the company is damaged or broken forever.

LISTENING TO COMPLAINTS

Listening carefully to complaints sends a signal to customers that your organization is customer focused. This says that you see customers as partners and as the reason for your business; therefore, you want to build relationships with them. Your organization's culture should support customers as a part of the business, making it much more likely to encourage an open and honest response from them.

Most of us ask for feedback that is likely to result in a positive or at least a neutral response. This happens when we ask questions such as, "Are you finding everything all right?" (asked by a department store salesperson) or "How was your meal?" (asked by a restaurant waitress). These kinds of questions are likely to get responses such as, "Yes, I'm finding things okay" or "The food is just

fine," whether or not everything really is fine. Your questions could
be rephrased in a way that yields more information; for example, if
the salesclerk asks, "How may I help you?" or the waitress in the
restaurant example asks, "What can I do to improve your meal?"
they are likely to get a more helpful reply.

MANAGEMENT TIPS
FOR COMPLAINTS

Management can make customer complaints easier to get, too. Use
a complaint phone line where the customer won't be put on hold.
Use various methods of thanking customers for their remarks or
complaints. These can include the free products or meals already
mentioned, thank-you calls or notes, or some other type of recognition—even a "consultant of the month" award.

   Don't just collect complaints—do something about them! Do
what you can to correct the problem that customers are complaining about. Without that step, simply gathering the complaints is
meaningless. Once you develop this new attitude toward complaints, you'll probably develop new attitudes toward your non-
complaining customers, too. Your relations with them will improve—and so will your business.

Key Terms

bad news skills   customer   customer report
                         complaints   card

Review Questions

1. Have you found yourself in the position of the nice customer?
   Describe the situation. After reading this chapter, would you
   still be a "nice" customer in the same situation?
2. Suppose you are the owner of a small restaurant, and you
   would like to start using customer report cards to improve
   your business. What questions would you want customers to
   answer in these report cards? On what aspects of the business
   would you like them to comment?

3. Suppose you are the manager of a small retail store. How can you encourage complaints from your customers? Why would you want to?

4. Describe the steps you can take to develop good "bad news skills."

5. What is meant by the suggestion to rethink customer complaints?

Multiple Choice

1. Mark Rutland had been waiting 45 minutes for a haircut at the styling salon. The stylist said the wait would be less than 15 minutes. Now someone who came in after Mark has been called by the stylist. Mark's response as a "nice" customer is to:
   a. Smile, say "I've changed my mind," and leave.
   b. Politely tell the receptionist that he was there first.
   c. Gruffly ask for the manager so that he can file a complaint.
   d. Jump up and down, screaming that he's tired of being treated like an idiot.

2. Melanie Daniels would like to develop her "bad news skills." Which of the following steps is *not* a good idea in doing so:
   a. Be polite.
   b. Apologize over and over again.
   c. Explain why the problem happened.
   d. Suggest solutions.

3. When explaining to a customer *why* you can't refund her money for a dress she is returning, which of the following reasons should you *avoid* giving?
   a. "Because it is company policy."
   b. "Because you have worn it."
   c. "Because it was not purchased at this store."
   d. "Because you do not have a receipt or the original tags."

4. As a telephone salesperson, which of the following statements would be a good way to encourage customer complaints at the end of the phone call:
   a. "Thanks for your business, have a nice day."
   b. "Your order is now complete. Please call again."

c. "Thank you for calling. What can I do for you?"

   d. "What else can I do to help you today?"

5. A business might start offering a "consultant of the month" award in order to:

   a. Bring in outside consultants to tell customers news they don't want to hear.

   b. Reward sales consultants for bringing in the most new business.

   c. Encourage customer complaints.

   d. Identify and get rid of obnoxious customers.

Marnie's Manager

Marnie Edgar was the customer service representative on duty at a busy discount store. Her manager was watching over her shoulder, evaluating her, this particular day as a customer came in with a complaint.

Customer:	I got this combination rice cooker and vegetable steamer as a gift. I don't like it, and I want my money back.
Marnie:	Is there anything wrong with it?
Customer:	No, I told you! I don't like it! It doesn't work right!
Marnie:	If it's defective, you can go back and get another one, and I will exchange it for you.
Customer:	I *told* you! I just don't like it!
Marnie:	[*Politely*] Do you have your receipt? We're not allowed to give cash refunds without a receipt. It's company policy.
Customer:	Didn't I tell you it was a *gift?* I don't have the receipt!

As the customer's anger grew, so did the manager's annoyance . . . and Marnie's nervousness. I must be doing something wrong! she thought to herself, but what?

1. Why is Marnie's manager becoming annoyed? Is Marnie doing something wrong?
2. Rephrase Marnie's questions to the customer so that you encourage complaints and get as much information as possible.
3. How can Marnie change the outcome of this interaction in a way that increases the chance that the customer will return as a satisfied customer?

23

Giving Customers and Clients the Strokes They Need

Roberta Evans, an instructor at a small business college, was gathering her books and notes together after class one day. She was satisfied that today she had given one of her better lectures. But as she walked out of the room, she overhead two students talking about her and the class.

"She is so arrogant! If I give a wrong answer, she rolls her eyes and sighs as if I were some kind of idiot. She makes me feel so stupid!" said Jawan.

"No kidding!" said Zamir. "She never tries to makes us feel as though we did anything right, she never writes positive comments on our papers or tests, and she has to have total control of the class all the time. She doesn't care how we feel. She treats us like we're robots or something!"

Roberta thought to herself, Wow, I had no idea I had that effect on my students. I should know enough about self-esteem to know how important it is to students. I should be trying to build up my students' self-esteem, not tear it down! I'd better change my approach and start giving my students the strokes they need.

No matter what kind of business you are in—academics, fast food, sales, health care, manufacturing—somewhere there is a customer or a client you are serving. Learning how to treat other people so that you build up their self-esteem is also called "giving strokes." In this chapter, we will talk about how to give strokes to customers.

WHY GIVE STROKES?

Even if you do not serve customers or clients directly, this chapter can help you to improve your relations with co-workers and other people in general. We need to be aware of the self-esteem issue in all of our relationships with people, because all people need to have a healthy and positive self-image.

STEPS TO BUILD SELF-ESTEEM IN OTHERS

You can take five steps to build up your customers' self-esteem.

1. **Help the customer feel at ease.**   Getting your customer to relax and to feel at ease with you and with your company is the important first step. Smile! Make it a real smile, not a phony one—people can tell the difference. Use the customer's name when you speak to him or her, but don't use a first name until you know the customer better. Using a first name may show a lack of respect; some people may want only their close friends to call them by their first names. With these customers, you may never get on a first-name basis.

Stand far enough away from customers so that you don't invade their personal space and make them feel uncomfortable (in our culture, that distance is about three feet). Listen to the customers' tone of voice and rate of speaking, and watch for body language cues. Try to match their tone, rate of speech, and body language, but keep your own style—if you mimic other people too closely, they will think you are making fun of them. These may seem like subtle details, but we all tend to identify with people who are like us, including people with similar mannerisms.

If you have a customer, for example, who nods while you are talking to show that he is listening, do the same when he is talking. If you are talking to a client who speaks slowly and in a monotone, and your normal speech is fast and animated, slow down your speech and regulate the tone. These changes may seem strange to you, but after a few tries they will become easier and you may find yourself adjusting to other people's mannerisms without even realizing it.

2. **Put yourself in the customer's place.**   Try to feel **empathy,** or what it is like to be in the other person's place. Empathy is not the same as **sympathy,** which is feeling sorry for another person. Develop a habit of feeling empathy for other people by asking yourself, If I were this customer with his or her needs, how would I feel? This can be a difficult habit to learn. But if you start thinking this way, you will improve all of your human relationships, not just your customer relations.

Let's say you are a hospital administrator meeting with an unhappy spouse of a hospitalized patient. Your hospital's policy does not allow family members to stay overnight in the hospital with patients. But sitting in front of you is a very upset husband telling you that he has not spent a single night away from his wife in 37 years, and that she needs him with her while she is ill. You may feel sorry for him (sympathy), but that is not enough. Put yourself in his place (empathy). How does he feel? He is probably very worried about his wife, maybe even terrified, and not sure whether he can handle these stressors or whether his wife will be all right without him. What can you do to relieve his feelings?

3. **Help the customer feel as though you understand him or her.** Like everyone else, customers need to feel that they are communicating effectively. Be sure that you are interpreting what they say correctly. One way to do this is to develop a habit of paraphrasing what they say. Start a question with "Do you mean . . . ?" or "It sounds like you are saying that . . ." This lets the customer know that you care enough to listen and to understand what he is saying. Don't be afraid to ask enough questions so that you are sure about what they are saying and that they understand what you are saying.

Let's say that you sell manufactured homes. You are listening to customers explain why the color scheme that you selected to show them (teal with pink trim) may not be quite what they had in mind. They are nodding and smiling and seem to be agreeing that it is a nice color combination, but at the same time they might be saying that they don't like it. You are not sure if they are politely telling you that it is a terrible color combination, or if they are still deciding whether they like the home or not. A good question to ask might be, "Are you saying that you really don't care for this color, and that you would prefer to look at a different color scheme?"

4. **Help the customer feel important.**   One of the best ways to improve all kinds of relationships is to make other people feel that they are the most important people you are talking to, at least right at the moment. One of the worst things you can do is to allow distractions, such as phone calls or other people walking in, to pull your concentration away from customers. This makes them feel that you do not value their business (or in personal relationships, that you do not value their friendship). To the customer, you are the whole company. Do everything you can to make that feeling go both ways.

Suppose that while you are meeting with a client in your office, a co-worker bursts in to ask if he can borrow your computer manual. You must show your client that she is more important by saying, "I'm sorry, Dan, I can't get that for you right now, I'm meeting with someone. I'll drop it by your office when I'm finished here."

5. **Praise the customer in an appropriate way.**   You may not have to look very far to see what people would like to receive **praise** for. Is there a picture of the customer's family on the desk? Compliment him on it. Has the customer accomplished something important or special recently? Congratulate her for it.

Praise can be a powerful tool in all human relationships, not only in the workplace. But it must be used in a real and caring way. Praise that is insincere is worse than no praise at all. Be specific in giving praise. Don't just tell Teresa, "Hey, nice work!" Instead, tell her, "Great job organizing the open house last week! Everything went really well!" If you don't have specific information about the situation, ask a specific question in a nonthreatening way. For example, "Teresa, I heard the open house last week went really well. How many people showed up?" If the compliment is too general, the customer can be left wondering, "What was that all about?" A specific question shows real interest and can lead to a point of information for which you can give sincere praise. For example, when Teresa tells you how many people came to the open house, this gives you enough information to say something like, "Wow! That's a lot more people than last year! You must really be getting the information out!"

GIVING STROKES FOR SELF-ESTEEM

It is worth repeating: Leaving customers with good feelings is very important. Treating customers as if they are the most important part of your business organization will pay off in the long run. Repeat business is a big part of any business, and it is easier to get than recruiting new customers. Unhappy customers will hurt your business in the long run. People who are not happy with your service will tell others, which will in turn reduce the number of your customers.

If you help customers to be happy with themselves by following the suggestions for building their self-esteem or giving them strokes, they will be quicker to warm up to you and to accept what you are saying (or selling) to them. If you get wrapped up in trying to impress customers, you will miss the mark. We all need to feel comfortable, to feel that we are understood by other people, and to feel that we are important to other people.

Key Terms

"giving strokes"   empathy   praise

feel at ease   sympathy

Review Questions

1. Why is it important to build self-esteem in others?
2. Have you found yourself (as a customer, client, or student) being treated in a way that made you feel unimportant, or as if the other person wasn't listening to you? Explain the situation. What could the other person have done differently for a better outcome?
3. Referring to the situation in question 2, what could you have done differently (as the client) to make the other person realize you weren't feeling at ease or understood?
4. Have you found yourself in a position where you needed to listen to another person and treat that person with empathy, but you felt annoyed or impatient instead? Explain the situation. What could you have done differently for a better outcome?

5. Think of a situation in which you have an ongoing relationship with another person (a co-worker, a family member), but the two of you haven't been communicating well lately. Describe the situation. How could you praise that person? Practice delivering the compliment or praise.

Multiple Choice

1. Steven is a clerk at a sporting goods store. He is usually rude and impatient with customers. A probable outcome of his attitude is that:
   a. He will lose current customers.
   b. He may lose his job.
   c. He will lose future customers.
   d. All of the above.

2. A first step in getting your customers to relax and feel comfortable with you is to:
   a. Use the customer's first name right away.
   b. Stand within one foot from the person to show you are friendly.
   c. Smile and be friendly.
   d. Act solemn and straight-faced, so the customer knows you are serious.

3. Your veterinarian takes time to talk to you when you bring your puppy in for shots. She asks questions like "Are you saying that . . . ?" and "Are you concerned about . . . ?" She has learned an important way to:
   a. Give praise.
   b. Help you feel as though she understands you.
   c. Make you feel important.
   d. Help you feel at ease and relaxed.

4. When Demitrius goes to see his professor to find out why his paper earned a failing grade, his professor said "I'm sorry for you, but I don't understand how any college student could write so poorly." The professor is showing a *lack* of:
   a. Empathy
   b. Sympathy
   c. Apathy
   d. Telepathy

5. You make an appointment to see your boss to ask for a raise.

During the appointment, she takes several phone calls and ends the meeting early, saying she has an urgent appointment elsewhere. By doing this, she forgot the rule of:

a. Making you feel at ease.
b. Praising you.
c. Putting herself in your place.
d. Helping you feel important.

Time for a Job, or No Job This Time?

Sam is interviewing for a job as a physical therapy assistant at a big hospital in San Francisco. He arrives at his appointment on time, dressed in his new suit, excited about the possibility of his first real job since graduation. When the personnel interviewer, Terry, walks in, Sam notices that he is carrying a stack of applications that look just like Sam's. Terry is also 15 minutes late. Without looking at Sam directly, Terry asks him to have a seat. Terry begins the interview, during which he looks at his watch several times, answers a few phone calls, and shuffles through the stack of applications. He frowns at some of Sam's answers, and looks out the window a lot.

By the time the interview is over, Sam is exhausted, uncomfortable, and very upset. As he leaves the hospital, he mutters to himself, "What happened here? What kind of interview was that? I'm not sure I'd want to take this job, even if they offered it to me."

1. What went wrong at this interview, and why is Sam so upset about it?

2. What clues tell you that Terry made Sam feel ill at ease, unimportant, or misunderstood? What could Terry have done differently? Could Sam have done anything differently to help this situation?

3. If you were in Terry's place, how could you have praised Sam appropriately? How could you have shown empathy?

24

Becoming the Leader of a Team

Hal Lincoln was overjoyed when management chose him to be the new team leader in the bottling company where he had worked for three years. By the end of the second week in his new role, however, he noticed that he was having trouble getting the seven people on his team to see him as a leader. He was often interrupted during team meetings by team members who were impatient to be heard. Hal's suggested methods of approaching problems were often ignored. "We don't seem to have any real teamwork on this team," Hal told his manager. "I don't even feel like a team member, let alone a leader."

"Well," his manager replied, "We'd better change that right away. Come to my office this afternoon, and I'll get you lined up for some leadership training."

What types of important skills should Hal learn in his forthcoming training? What do you need to know to keep from falling into the trap of producing a leaderless team? Leadership in today's world is constantly changing. The skills required for team leadership in the 1990s are not the same as those needed a generation ago.

The terms *leadership* and *management* are often confused. Leadership refers to a person's ability to influence others toward the fulfillment of goals. Management refers to the performance of the four functions of all managers—planning, organizing, influencing, and controlling. Both in traditional leadership and in team leadership, a manager is not necessarily a leader.

FORMAL AND INFORMAL LEADERS AND POWER

If you have been selected as a team leader, you are the formal leader. Your effectiveness, though, will be determined greatly by your acceptance by the team as the informal leader. The positions of formal and informal leader are not necessarily held by the same people. Often, a formal leader's power will be undercut by an informal leader who has no authority in the organization—only power. Let's look at the differences between power and authority, as we examine the differing roles of the formal and the informal leader.

Sources of Power

Power is the ability to influence people, decisions, and events. Experts have identified six different sources of power, or ways that a person can gain power in a group or organization:

1. Reward power. This source of power comes from a person's ability to give positive rewards such as security or money. For **reward power** to be significant, the leader must be seen by others as someone who controls such rewards.

2. Coercive power.   This power is based on the fear that the leader can punish the follower for not doing things his or her way. In many ways, **coercive power** is the opposite of reward power. It could be called punishment power. One major difference between the two is that the perceived punishment does not ever have to take place, as long as the fear that it will take place can change the followers' attitudes or behavior. As with reward power, the leader must be seen by others as someone who controls the potential punishment.

3. Control-of-information. This source of power is a kind of knowledge power. It comes from having knowledge that other people don't have. Some people use **control-of-information power** by sharing and withholding information in order to control others.

4. Referent power. This power is based on "that special something" that some people seem to have. **Referent power** is variously labeled charisma, charm, likable personality, and several other traits that draw other people to those who have it.

5. Expert power.   This source of power comes from the leader's expertise in an area that directly affects a related area where the leader wants to influence people. An example of **expert power** is a small company in which only one or two people can operate the computer system. The expert's ability with the computer system allows him or her power in areas beyond those directly related to the system.[1] Perhaps the expert will choose not to take advantage of this power that the expertise allows. It is there for the leader's use—and sometimes as a temptation.

Do you recognize yourself as having access to one of these areas of power? If so, are you using that source ethically and to the best of your ability? If not, are you sure that you couldn't cultivate one or more of them? Also, do you recognize that members of your organization use these power sources? How can an awareness of their use of power help you better understand them and their roles in the group?

Once you find that you have power, how should you use it? Some leaders are afraid that if leadership power is "spread around," it will be less effective, leaving the leader in a somewhat helpless position. One of the best ways you can use power effectively is to share it with the team. When done correctly, delegating power simply enforces your power by having more people buy into it. After all, power is worth little without others. If others become involved in *using* the power, they will also be more willing—and useful—followers.

THE TEAM APPROACH TO THE USE OF POWER

A team leader's goal is team performance. Unlike traditional work groups whose success depends on the individual performance of each member, teams should attempt to reach goals that are above those that they could accomplish as separate units. The team leader has the task of blending the skills of the group into a kind of collective skill. This process should also produce group-centered accountability. The victories and near victories should be valued by

---

[1] Excerpted from J. R. P. French, Jr. and Bertram Raven, "The Bases of Social Power," in *Studies in Social Power*, D. Cartwright, ed. (Ann Arbor: MI: Institute for Social Research, 1959).

the group as a whole, and the defeats—if any—should be seen as group defeats. If blame for shortcomings has to be placed at all, it should be placed on the whole group.

How can you as a leader be the kind of person who can bring about this level of teamwork? The key word is *attitude*. Traditional leaders often think they are expected to have the answers. A team leader must adopt the attitude that he or she doesn't have all the answers—and that not having the answers is often the best way to lead. The answers need to come from the group as a whole for the team approach to work. However, you need also to know when to be the decision-maker. In their best-selling book, *The Wisdom of Teams*, Katzenbach and Smith say: "team performance almost always depends on how well team leaders . . . strike a critical balance between doing things themselves and letting other people do them."[2]

This delicate balance must be maintained at all times for team leadership to be successful. Because each team is different, though, no blanket rules exist for all groups and situations. Some teams will need a great deal of direction while others will seem to run themselves. Also, few teams are static; they grow and develop. As they grow, the role of the leader needs to change. Be alert to the changes. One important characteristic to watch for is the growing self-confidence of members as the group moves through new victories and accomplishments.

DUTIES OF THE TEAM LEADER

Among the duties of the team leader are to serve as the communication link between the team and the organization, and also as the record keeper of the team's goals, accomplishments, agendas, budgets (if any), and important communications. Above all, the team leader is an official and complete member of the team. As such, the leader also must be conscientious about attending group meetings, carrying out assignments outside of meetings, and generally sharing in the team's work.[3]

---

[2] J. R. Katzenbach and D. K. Smith, *The Wisdom Of Teams* (New York: HarperCollins, 1994), p. 131.

[3] Peter R. Scholtes, et al., *The Team Handbook: How to Use Teams to Improve Quality* (Madison, WI: Joiner Associates, 1992), pp. 3–10.

As a team leader, you must carefully examine your attitude toward power, especially if you previously have been a leader in a nonteam setting. Experts in quality teams tell us that problems that develop are not usually the fault of any one person, but are caused in some way by the system. Get into the habit of stepping back and taking a few deep breaths before placing blame for problems on anyone. This includes unduly blaming yourself as the leader. Energy is much more effective when focused on solutions; look to perfecting the processes of the group to prevent future problems in the same areas.

Here are some additional tips for effective team leadership:[4]

1. Be real.   One of the most useful points for team leaders to remember is to be themselves. If the group is going to feel secure and confident, all members must feel good about who is leading them. Any group will pick up very quickly on phoniness and insincerity.

2. Speak and listen clearly, carefully, and empathically.   Be direct; make sure everyone understands what you are saying. Use frequent perception checks during meetings with the team. Ask questions such as, "Do you all understand what I'm trying to say?" and "Please, if you don't follow me completely on this, ask questions."

3. Show that you care.   Your attitude should communicate respect for the dignity of all group members. Respect is a two-way street. Showing respect toward the group will heighten the respect they show toward you.

4. Learn to unify and summarize fragmented ideas.   A team will frequently offer ideas that are parts of a whole. The bigger picture that unifies them may seem to be an abstract and untouchable concept. One of your jobs as team leader is to pull those ideas together, showing their relationships to each other and to the goals of the group.

5. Create a climate where disagreement is acceptable.   Encourage minority opinions. It is often easy to get caught in the trap of discouraging discord. In the process, leaders sometimes find themselves discouraging opinions that may be contrary to those of the majority. Minority opinions have been known to save the very existence of groups. Don't be a judge; stay objective and allow opinions within the team to focus.

---

[4] Based in part on *Facilitating Effective Teams* (Wilsonville, OR: Oregon Advanced Technology Consortium, 1994), and Katzenbach and Smith, pp. 141–43.

6. **Ask good questions.** The questions you ask as a team leader are often more important than the statements you make. Open-ended questions are often the best because they allow the members to explore creative avenues that you as the leader might not have examined or even thought of.

7. **Use positive statements of praise.** Whenever a good idea is presented, praise it sincerely. Celebrate successes, even small ones. A positive, accepting climate produces greater levels of creativity.

8. **Balance patience with the need to take charge.** As the leader, you need to lead. However, let the group discover as many things for themselves as possible. This approach requires patience. But when command decisions need to be made, make them.

9. **Manage relationships with those outside of the team.** As the leader of the team, you are the channel to the rest of the company and the rest of the world. Don't ever betray the trust of the group to outsiders. Managing relationships includes communicating the needs, goals, and purpose of the group to others in an accurate and realistic manner.

Becoming an effective team leader requires skills that almost anyone can achieve. Following these guidelines will help you in the process. Read all you can on the function of teams; many good books and articles on the subject are now available. You can become an effective team leader if you stay focused on your goals and facilitate the group's progress.

Key Terms

leadership

management

formal leader

informal leader

sources of power:

  reward power

coercive power

control-of-
  information
  power

referent power

expert power

team approach

duties of the team
  leader

tips for effective
  team leadership

Review Questions

1. What is *power?* What methods of gaining and maintaining power have you observed in your lifetime?

2. What are some helpful tips for someone who wants to become an effective team leader?
3. How is a team leader's function different from that of a traditional leader?
4. One of the tips for becoming an effective team leader is to create a climate where disagreement is acceptable. Why would you want disagreement as part of team leadership?
5. An effective team leader must always maintain a balance between letting the team control itself and directing its decisions. Comment on the importance of that balance and how it can be maintained.

Multiple Choice

1. Which of the following statements is correct?
   a. The terms *leadership* and *management* mean the same thing.
   b. Power is a sinister force and is always misused by leaders.
   c. Power is the ability to influence people, decisions, and events.
   d. Leadership skills are talents one is born with, not learned from training.
2. A team leader's goal is to:
   a. Use power to achieve his or her own agendas.
   b. Get team performance results from the team.
   c. Listen, but not to talk.
   d. Make sure the group is always in harmony, never arguing about issues.
3. Which of the following is *not* one of the sources of power identified by experts?
   a. Argumentative power
   b. Control-of-information power
   c. Coercive power
   d. Expert power
4. As the needs of the team change:
   a. The leader must be sure to stand his or her ground and not change with the team.
   b. The leader should examine the leadership role and change it when necessary.
   c. The leader should bring in someone from the outside to find out why the change is taking place.

    d. The team members need to find a new leader who reflects those changes.

5. Which of the following is *not* one of the duties of the team leader?

    a. The record keeper of the team's goals.

    b. The communication link between the team and the organization.

    c. To be an official and complete member of the team.

    d. The idea person who produces concepts for the future.

The Problem at Amalgamated

Amalgamated of Prineville is a wood-products company that specializes in hardwood flooring and decorative paneling. The company has just established the team concept companywide. Lucy Burton was appointed the team leader for her research and development area.

Lucy feels strongly that Amalgamated is too dependent on the home building industry for sales. During the past 15 years, the company has been forced to lay off workers whenever a downturn occurred in the regional economy because new housing starts would always decrease during a recession. Lucy is convinced that the company should start producing products that are independent of the construction business and its whims.

She has led her team accordingly. By the time the first team meeting was over, Lucy had convinced eight of the ten members of her group to present top management with a plan for the manufacture of a line of oak furniture. After the meeting, she spent long hours with the two dissenting team members, trying to win them over. By the next meeting, only one person thought Lucy's idea was wrong.

1. Was Lucy Burton using effective team leadership? Why or why not?

2. What could the dissenting members (or any other member) do to change the way things are being done in this team?

3. Is it possible that the new furniture line might be successful? If so, what's wrong with this case?

YOUR SKILLS AND SPECIAL ISSUES
IN HUMAN RELATIONS

PART Three

III

25

Chapter

Drugs, Alcohol, the Workplace, and You

"Now what?" groaned Jim to his best friend, Lionel, at work one day. "If the plant starts doing random drug testing like the foreman says, I'll get fired for sure. If I go over to the new plant, they won't do random drug testing after I get hired, but I'd have to pass the drug test in order to get hired. What's the point? Maybe I'll just quit working, and get unemployment."

"Hey, here's a thought," said Lionel in a teasing tone, even though he was dead serious, "why don't you just give up the drugs and get clean?"

"Lionel, you know I've tried. I just can't seem to make it on my own! So now what?"

It's true that from time to time, we all have personal problems that affect our work. Some of these problems may involve drugs or alcohol. How we handle these problems affects our future careers as well as our personal lives. We are all responsible for handling our own personal problems effectively—as workers, as managers, or in any other role. These problems can be very serious, but they do not need to ruin our careers or our lives. In this chapter, we will talk about some of the problems that happen when drugs or alcohol are brought into our work lives, and what to do about these situations.

EMPLOYEE ASSISTANCE PROGRAMS

In the story above, Jim is assuming that he has to handle his drug problem by himself, but the idea of doing this is so overwhelming that he wouldn't know where to start. This is why **Employee Assistance Programs (EAPs)** were started in the 1940s. Along with the Alcoholics Anonymous program, the first EAPs were designed to help employees who had problems with alcohol. In the 1960s, EAPs were expanded to treat employees with other drug problems as well as other life problems, such as marital, family, and financial problems.

For EAPs to work, supervisors have to be willing and able to observe employees, watch for problems, confront the problems by referring employees to EAPs, and then follow through to see that employees seek out the programs. Employees who are referred to EAPs are usually told that their involvement is voluntary, and that they are free to reject the help. With or without the EAP help, though, their jobs will depend on their future performance. Thus, without taking advantage of the help from EAPs, employees could lose their jobs. EAPs benefit employees by providing them with a chance for rehabilitation. They benefit employers by improving attendance and safety records, and reducing health care costs. A good EAP program helps everyone involved!

ALCOHOL AND DRUG ABUSE

Alcohol and drug abuse, or **substance abuse,** is one of the most common employee problems that employers face. It is also one of the most expensive, costing U.S. businesses close to $200 billion dollars a year.[1] These costs include estimates for lost productivity in the workplace due to alcohol-related illnesses and accidents, health care costs, and treatment costs. No business is immune to substance abuse because an estimated 95 percent of alcoholics and 70 percent of drug abusers work part or full time.

---

[1] From the National Council on Alcoholism and Drug Dependence, in "Alcoholism Has a High Cost," *H R Focus,* Aug. 1993, p. 8.

Understanding Substance Abuse

When we think of substance abuse, we usually think of illegal drugs such as cocaine or marijuana. But legal drugs can be abused, too, both prescription drugs such as tranquilizers and over-the-counter drugs such as diet pills. So can substances that we don't normally think of as drugs at all, such as nicotine and caffeine. But the most dangerous legal drug of all, according to the American Medical Association, is alcohol.

When is a substance abused?   What qualifies as drug abuse depends more on the effects of the substance and how a person uses it than on its legality or illegality. Any substance that affects a person's judgment, behavior, mental processes, mood, conscious experience, or perceptions is called a **psychoactive drug.** There is no clear line where substance use stops and substance abuse begins. In general, substance abuse is happening when a person keeps on using the substance after it is causing problems in the person's life. These could include problems at school, at work, in a person's social life, physical health, or mental health. With abuse it is not the actual amount of the psychoactive drug that is the problem, but how much the drug is interfering with a person's life. For example, if a person misses classes or forgets an important appointment because he or she is drunk or hung over, then abuse is happening.

Dependence.   More serious and more severe than abuse is **dependence,** but again, there is no clear line between the two. A person who has **withdrawal symptoms** (painful physical symptoms when the drug is not being used) or whose abuse leads to **tolerance** (needing more and more of a substance to get the desired effects) is experiencing **physical dependence.** A person who craves the drug and organizes his or her life around getting more of it and using it is said to have a **psychological dependence.** A person who is experiencing physical or psychological dependence has lost control over the substance. Another term often used to describe dependence is **addiction.**

fit for duty
exam

Recognizing Substance Abuse in the Workplace

Recognizing substance abuse and identifying substance abusers can be difficult. Substance abusers are found in all occupational groups, among both sexes, and in all ethnic or racial groups. But there are ways to recognize who is abusing substances, including changes in a person's appearance—the **physical signs** of substance abuse, or changes in the way a person acts—the **behavioral signs** of substance abuse.

Physical signs of substance abuse.

1. Slurred speech
2. Bloodshot eyes.
3. An unsteady walk.
4. The smell of alcohol or marijuana on a person.

Behavioral signs of substance abuse.

1. Missing work often.
2. Coming in to work late or leaving early.
3. Taking long coffee breaks or lunch breaks.
4. Irritability or other personality changes.
5. Avoiding supervisors and co-workers.
6. Having conflicts with co-workers or supervisors.
7. Blaming others when things go wrong.
8. Feeling resentful or "picked on."
9. Lowered job performance or efficiency, or an increasing number of mistakes on the job.
10. Financial problems, or having wages withheld because of legal action.
11. Difficulty in recalling and following instructions on the job.
12. Repeated accidents off the job that affect job performance.
13. Loss of interest in normal appearance or grooming.
14. Chemically caused "blackouts" or memory loss.

15. Memory loss due to psychological reasons; losing memory of events that cause guilt or embarrassment.[2]

These two lists identify only some of the physical or behavioral signs of substance abuse, but a person may have only a few of these signs and still be a substance abuser. For these reasons, it is not always easy to spot an employee who is having substance abuse problems.

RESPONDING TO SUBSTANCE ABUSE IN THE WORKPLACE

Employer Substance Abuse Policies

Before managers or supervisors can do anything about substance abuse in the workplace, they have to develop a company policy on substance abuse and put it in place. This policy should state clearly what testing and search procedures will be used, if any. It also should state possible disciplinary actions that the company may take against employees who are substance abusers. This policy must be understood by and applicable to all levels of employees. Awareness and education campaigns should be part of this policy.

Managers or supervisors need to understand the policy so they know what they have to enforce. They need training in what illegal substances look like, what the characteristics of abusers are, and what EAP resources are available to employees. *Managers or supervisors should not try to be the employee's counselor!* Their job is only to refer employees to counseling, not to try to treat the employees themselves.

Substance abusers are often in denial; that is, they deny that they have a problem to themselves and to others. Supervisors should not accuse employees outright of being substance abusers, partly because the likely response will be denial and partly because of the possibility of legal action. The supervisor's main task is to

---

[2] Laura Lyons and Brian Kleiner, "Managing the Problem of Substance Abuse Without Abusing Employees," *H R Focus,* April 1992.

make sure that employees understand that their job performance is unacceptable, and that whatever is causing this poor performance must stop.

Employee Drug Testing

The **Drug-Free Work Place Act of 1988** says that certain types of businesses must take action to make their workplaces drug free. To comply with this act, employers often undertake drug testing. Testing employees for drug use is one of the most controversial issues in the workplace today. The controversy arises because of the Constitution's Fourth Amendment, which guarantees citizens the right to privacy against search and seizure activities. This right has to be balanced against the rights of businesses and private citizens to be free from drugs and substance abusers at work.

Drug testing can be a good way to prevent and detect substance abuse in the workplace, but if not handled properly it can lead to unhappy employees and lawsuits. Drug testing can lower company morale by giving employees the impression that their employers do not trust them. Employees may feel that they are under constant suspicion of drug use, when they may not use drugs at all.

Companies that choose to use drug testing may test employees only before hiring, or they may test randomly after an employee is hired. Some companies may fire employees the first time a positive test result comes back, and others may fire employees only as a last resort after EAP interventions have failed. Companies that use drug testing and identify substance abusers also have to be aware of Title VII of the amended Civil Rights Act of 1964, which states that discrimination against the handicapped is illegal, and most states define substance abuse *recovery* as a lifelong disability or handicap.

WHEN SUBSTANCE ABUSE LEADS TO OTHER PROBLEMS

Substance abuse is often tied, in a vicious cycle, to other personal problems. For example, an employee may be going through a bitter divorce and child custody suit. Because of the stress, grief, and depression, this employee may turn to alcohol or other drugs to ease these painful emotions. Before long, this employee may abuse the substance and then become dependent on it. The substance abuse in turn can lead to other personal problems. For example, the employee may start having serious financial problems as a result of buying the substance or losing a job because of the substance abuse. These problems can also be helped by EAPs.

HOW TO INTERVENE IN EMPLOYEE PERSONAL OR SUBSTANCE ABUSE PROBLEMS

If your job includes recognizing and stepping in when employees are having substance abuse problems or personal problems, here are some steps you can take to intervene.

1. **Observe.** Carefully observe the employee's behavior to understand how the job performance has changed.
2. **Open the door to communication.** Give employees an opportunity to talk about their problems in a nonthreatening way.
3. **Create trust.** Create an atmosphere of trust and concern for the employee by listening carefully and with empathy.
4. **Encourage action.** Encourage the employee to take some action, such as getting counseling.
5. **Develop a plan.** Guide the employee toward developing a plan of action to reduce the effects of the problem at work.
6. **Follow up.** Follow up to provide ongoing support to the employee.
7. **Be patient.** Keep in mind that problems may take a long time to resolve. Be willing to listen and help the employee stay committed to change.[3]

No matter what your role is at your place of employment, help is available for these types of problems. Resources are available to managers and supervisors for help in managing personal and substance abuse problems.

---

[3] Clinton Longnecker and Dennis Kale, "When Marital Problems Come to Work," *Supervisory Management*, 36, pp. 6–7.

Key Terms

Employee
  Assistance
  Programs (EAPs)

substance abuse

psychoactive drug

dependence

withdrawal
  symptoms

tolerance

physical
  dependence

psychological
  dependence

addiction

physical signs of
  substance abuse

behavioral signs of
  substance abuse

denial

Drug-Free Work
  Place Act of 1988

Review Questions

1. Does the company you work for have a substance abuse policy? If so, what does it say? If you don't know, how could you find out?
2. Is there an EAP at your workplace? Do you know what the program provides employees? If not, how could you find out?
3. What is the difference between withdrawal, tolerance, and dependence?
4. What are some of the physical signs of substance abuse? behavioral signs?
5. Other than the substances discussed in this chapter, what other substances fit the definition of a psychoactive drug? Why do they fit?

Multiple Choice

1. Tippi constantly thinks about when she will be able to get her next drink. This is a sign of:
   a. Psychological dependence on alcohol.
   b. Physical dependence on alcohol.
   c. Tolerance to alcohol.
   d. Withdrawal from alcohol.
2. Random drug testing of employees in the workplace can lead to:
   a. Low morale.

b. Identifying substance abusers.

c. Mistrust of employers.

d. All of the above.

3. Which of the following is *not* recommended as a way for managers to handle substance abusers?

a. Encourage the employee to develop a plan of action.

b. Counsel and give therapy to the employee.

c. Refer the employee to the company's EAP.

d. Watch for physical and behavioral changes in the employee.

4. An EAP is likely to help employees with:

a. Financial problems.

b. Marital or family problems.

c. Substance abuse problems.

d. All of the above.

5. Employees who are undergoing rehabilitation for substance abuse recovery cannot be discriminated against because of:

a. Their company's EAP.

b. Amendments to the Civil Rights Act.

c. The Drug-Free Work Place Act.

d. Employee substance abuse policies.

Case 25–1

Spiraling Out of Control

Mariette was talking to Suzanne, her supervisor, in Suzanne's office after work one day.

Mariette: I just don't know what to do, Suzanne! My husband Rod lost his job last month after his company was bought out. He's really depressed, and he's started drinking again. Our savings are used up. I just can't seem to concentrate at work anymore! I'm so worried for him! What is he going to do to get some help? Since he's not working, there's no Employee Assistance Program he can go to! It just seems like everything is spinning out of control!

Suzanne: Mariette, right now, I'm more worried about you.
There *is* an EAP here for you, and you need it right
now! Let's go down to the human resources office.

1. Why does Suzanne say that Mariette is the one who needs the
EAP? What kind of EAP referrals would Suzanne benefit from?

2. How have Rod's problems become a vicious cycle? What kind of
problems does he need help for?

3. Suppose that you are in Suzanne's position. Now that Mariette has
opened the door to communication with you, what steps should
you take next?

26

What Should You Do about Those Troublemakers?

Lela and her Aunt Becky were reading the menu at a restaurant where they had met for dinner.

Lela: It's really nice that you could meet me on such short notice, Aunt Becky. I didn't know until this morning that the company would be sending me into town for those meetings.

Aunt Becky: I was glad I could make it, too. Now let's order. [*The waitress comes to take their orders*] I'd like the potato cheddar soup to start with. And a green salad. Do you have bleu cheese dressing?

Waitress: Yes, we do, but the dinner entrees come with soup *or* salad, and our soup today is French onion.

Aunt Becky: Well then, substitute the potato cheddar soup for the French onion, and give me the salad anyway! [*Disgusted*] And I'd like the prime rib. Give me the rice pilaf instead of the baked potato.

| Waitress: | I'm sorry, ma'am, but as you can see on the menu, we don't have the prime rib today and we don't offer substitutions. Is there anything else on the menu that looks good to you? |
| Aunt Becky: | [*Loudly*] This is ridiculous! I can't get a decent meal here! I'm leaving! |

Lela rolled her eyes and sighed. Another fun night going out to dinner with her aunt. She smiled at the waitress apologetically; Lela knew what a difficult customer her aunt could be.

Whether your troublemakers are customers or co-workers, there are strategies for dealing with difficult people to make your life easier. In this chapter, we'll discuss some of those strategies.

THE CUSTOMER IS ALWAYS RIGHT— MAYBE?

We've all heard the saying, "The customer is always right." Is this really true? Definitely, if you're talking about the kind of attitude it expresses. There are times when customers are very wrong, but your job is still to treat customers as if the way they see things is correct. This kind of attitude is going to require a lot of self-discipline on your part—not to mention some courage.

There are two things to remember when you are dealing with an angry or unreasonable customer. First, stay focused. The success of your company in the long term depends on satisfied customers. Second, avoid the **self-esteem trap.** Whatever the customer is upset about, it probably doesn't have much to do with you directly. But even if the problem is because of your mistakes, don't take the attack personally. Tell yourself that this is just business, it's not personal. Sometimes your best bet in getting a solution started is simply to get the customer calmed down.

HANDLE THE DIFFICULT CUSTOMER PROFESSIONALLY

Here are some easy-to-follow guidelines for dealing with a **difficult customer** who is already angry.

1. Let the customer vent his or her anger. Allow an angry customer to speak his or her mind. Even though this might be difficult, being a good listener is still the best approach. Cutting the customer off usually makes the customer more angry. Let the customer know you are sympathetic. When the customer has strong emotions, he or she needs a "sounding board."

2. Get all the facts. If it's possible, have the information on the case right in front of you. If the customer's story doesn't agree with the file in front of you, make sure your sources are correct. Ask questions to verify what the customer is saying. Ask enough questions until you are satisfied that you know what really happened. If the customer is wrong, don't tell him or her that directly. Always focus on what can be done to solve the problem instead of placing blame.

3. Understand the customer's feelings. When someone is very angry, what they are saying can be confusing. Make sure you understand the main issue the customer is talking about. What you see as the main issue might not be what the customer meant. Knowing what is wrong in the customer's eyes can help you figure out what to do to make it right.

4. Suggest possible solutions. Be specific. Be clear. Be careful not to make promises that you might not be able to keep. If the solution you come up with isn't enough to satisfy the customer, explain why you have to offer this solution instead of what the customer wanted. But try not to use "company policy" as an excuse if you don't have to. If you do, explain why there is such a policy.

5. End on a positive note. Once you have agreed to a solution, thank the customer for his or her patience and for bringing the problem to your attention. Don't apologize too much. Focus your attention on the future. Explain the steps the company is taking so that this type of problem doesn't happen again. Feel free to mention things you will do personally to prevent the problem from happening again. Your main goal now is to keep the customer's future business.

6. You can't win them all! Be as patient, empathic, and helpful as you can. Even when you are all of those things, you will sometimes have customers who remain angry and out for trouble. Some customers are difficult people who will stay that way no matter what anyone does. These people are troublemakers for any company.

Again, don't take their words or actions personally. If you need to, get help from your manager.

When the time comes to use these steps at your workplace, do the best you can. If you don't remember all six steps, at least remember this: Do whatever you can to keep an angry customer's complaint from turning into an argument. It take two people to argue. As the representative of your company, it's up to you to refuse to be the second person. You may have to bite your tongue a few times, but in the end your self-control will pay off.

BE ETHICAL

Acting in an ethical way is necessary in all dealings with customers. When you are deciding on an ethical approach to a situation, ask yourself, Would I want everything I have done in this situation to be public information? If your answer is no, you are not acting ethically.

Another guideline to follow is the Golden Rule. Are you treating the customer the way you would want to be treated? If you follow the philosophy that the customer's needs are the most important needs, then the ethics issue will take care of itself.

PROBLEM PEOPLE IN AN ORGANIZATION

Customers aren't the only problem people that have to be dealt with. Some **problem people at work** are the people you see every day. People cause problems when they don't live up to the organization's expectations. People who often cause problems at work include low conformers, jealous people, whiners, and passive people. We will talk about all of these types of people.

Low Conformers

Most of us are **high conformers** at work; that is, we like to fit in, we work well in teams, we are usually friendly, and we follow group norms and policies. **Low conformers** are just the opposite. They think independently and solve problems in a creative way, but in the process they cause some conflict. Other workers may find the low conformer's way of doing things to be chaotic and unfair to the

other employees who play by the rules. Some suggestions follow
for working with low conformers to make them less of a problem:

1. **Learn to tolerate their honesty.** Low conformers are usually open and straightforward, but they often lack the tact
   and diplomacy the rest of us are used to.

2. **Accept their self-expression.** Their self-expression might
   seem like stubbornness or disloyalty, but it probably isn't
   meant that way.

3. **Accept their independence.** Don't be offended if they
   don't ask for your advice or take advice when it's offered.

4. **Resist asking them to come to conclusions.** They may
   not be thinking about the outcome in the same way you
   are.

5. **Give positive reinforcement even when they don't seem
   to need it.** Make sure your reinforcement is relevant and
   sincere. All of us need encouragement. With these suggestions in mind, don't expect to change the personality of the
   low conformer any more than you can expect to change
   that of the high conformer. They balance each other out.

Jealous People

Jealous people want what other people have. They may feel suspicious and untrusting of others. These bad feelings can damage the
morale and productivity of the workplace. The following are suggestions for dealing with jealous people at work. Some of them may
seem to contradict each other, so you may need to try whichever
seems more appropriate in your situation or try more than one until
one works.

1. **Avoid destructive conflict with the jealous person.** This
   will help keep your actions more focused and purposeful.

2. **Confront the jealous co-worker.** The best way to deal with
   some people is to call them openly on their jealousy. This
   changes the game, giving you a power advantage. The jealous worker will probably back away and choose someone
   else as a target (you hope not another co-worker). A warning: Some jealous people will work hard behind your back
   to smear your name after a confrontation.

3. **Ignore the jealous person.** Be polite, say hello and good-bye, but don't start conversations. If the other person wants to chat, cut it short. Ignoring the jealous person gives you back some control and puts the other person off guard because the jealous person won't know where he or she stands.

4. **Talk the problem over with your manager.** This doesn't mean to start a gripe session or an open conflict. Your goal is more of a perception check: to check that your manager is seeing the other person's attitude in the same way you are.

Whatever you decide to do about a jealous person, don't lower yourself to the same level. Stay away from insults and backstabbing to get even. If you wait long enough, the problem will usually go away. Don't add fuel to the fire. Let the jealousy burn itself out.

Whiners and Complainers

Venter

Some people are never happy at work, and want to make sure everyone else knows about it. Whether you are their manager or a co-worker, here are steps you can take to deal with **whiners and complainers.**

1. **Listen, but not too much.** Don't let whiners and complainers take advantage of your sympathetic ear. Listen to an honest and relevant complaint about you, but put an end to a general gripe session.

2. **Do some reality checks.** Call the whiner's bluff by asking exactly what the problem is and what the person wants you to do about it.

3. **Challenge the complaint "unfair!"** Since childhood, we like to call a situation "unfair" when we don't get our way. Ask for specific facts and examples of unfairness.

4. **Be a team leader or player.** Promote teamwork and camaraderie. As a manager, explain the possibility of transfer for people who won't be team players. As a team member, be the kind of person who doesn't tolerate whiners. Whiners and complainers are problems waiting to happen.

Passive, Unresponsive People

These people can be the most difficult people to work with because
they seem to be agreeable and easygoing. **Passive, unresponsive
people** react to any confrontation or conflict by shutting down.
Being a quiet person is not the same as being passive. Some quiet
people will speak up when they have something important to say,
while others will screen out whatever is irrelevant and appear to be
unresponsive. Passive people, though, have different reasons for
not speaking up. Some use their lack of response as a way of taking
control and being aggressive (the silent treatment), others are in-
timidated and afraid of sounding stupid, and others are trying to
escape responsibility. Once you are convinced that you are dealing
with passive people, you can take some steps to get feedback from
them.

1. **Ask open-ended questions.**   Don't ask yes or no questions. Ask questions to which the passive person needs to
   give a longer answer. These questions encourage them to
   open up.
2. **Wait.**   After asking an open-ended question, look directly
   at the passive person with an expectant, quizzical expression. Develop and use a friendly, silent, stare. This expression should not be threatening. Wait for an answer longer
   than a merely comfortable pause.
3. **Don't fill in the space.**   Don't make small talk and don't
   rescue passive people. Sometimes they need time to orga-
   nize their thoughts.
4. **Help break the tension.**   Make open statements that call
   attention to what's going on. Ask questions such as, "Can
   you talk about why you're having a hard time answering?" or "You don't need to start at the beginning. What's
   on your mind now?"
5. **Set time limits.**   Plan in advance how much time you will
   spend dealing with the passive person and tell that person
   what this time limit is. Sometimes, the person will say
   what he or she needs to say in the last minutes of the conversation.

There may be other types of difficult people in the workplace than have been discussed here. To deal with them, you will need patience, good listening skills, and time. When a conflict starts, plan your strategy. Once you identify the problem, work toward a solution and try to get a commitment from the person. Most difficult people will never completely stop being difficult. Deal with their difficulties one at a time.

Key Terms

self-esteem trap	low conformers	passive, unresponsive people
difficult customer	jealous people	
problem people at work	whiners and complainers	
high conformers		

Review Questions

1. Have you ever been the target of a jealous person at work? What was the issue? How did you handle it (or not)? How would you handle it now, after reading this chapter?

2. What is meant by the "self-esteem trap"? How can you avoid getting trapped in a conflict situation?

3. Are you a low conformer or a high conformer? What clues helped you decide? How do these two types of people balance each other at work?

4. How can you tell the difference between someone at work who is just quiet and shy, and someone who is passive or unresponsive? How can you draw out a passive person? Would you guess that this is a different process from drawing out a quiet or shy person? Why or why not?

5. Have you worked with people who are whiners and complainers? How do you tell a "real" whine from a general whining session? What should you do when the whining is about you?

Multiple Choice

1. Marcy is selling perfume at a department store when
   an angry customer comes up to the counter and
   yells at Marcy that she was overcharged and cheated of
   her change. Marcy says to herself, I'm so stupid. I'm a
   terrible clerk. I should quit. Marcy has become a victim of
   the:
   a. Self-concept burn
   b. Self-esteem trap
   c. Self-image bellyflop
   d. Self-perception double image

2. When you are dealing with a customer who is already angry,
   what step should you take?
   a. End on a negative note.
   b. Always come out of it as the winner.
   c. Solve the problem based on the information from the
      customer only, not information from your company.
   d. Be sure you understand the customer's feelings.

3. One step you should take in dealing with a whiner or
   complainer at work is to:
   a. Listen as long as the person wants you to.
   b. Do frequent reality checks.
   c. Agree that the situation was unfair to the whiner.
   d. Be a "free agent," not a team player.

4. In drawing out a passive or unresponsive person, a suggested
   step is:
   a. Ask open-ended questions, not yes or no questions.
   b. Avoid eye contact with the person.
   c. Don't let the conversation be filled with uncomfortable
      silences.
   d. Leave the time open so that the person can take as long as
      he or she likes to open up.

5. All of the following are ways of dealing with a jealous co-
   worker except:
   a. Discussing the problem with your manager.
   b. Ignoring the jealous person.
   c. Avoiding destructive conflict with the person.
   d. Avoiding openly confronting the jealous person.

A Raise, a Lawsuit, or . . . ?

Sean McKenzie and Sheila Jones both worked as administrators in a hospice in southern California. Sheila was Sean's direct supervisor. They had gone through many emotional and stressful situations at work, and they had become very close friends. One of the nurses at the hospice, Jenny Thompson, couldn't help noticing how close Sean and Sheila were. In the nurses' lounge, Jenny spent a lot of time complaining that the two of them seemed a little too close. Jenny even told one of the other nurses, Brenda Taylor, that she thought Sheila was giving Sean extra brownie points toward a promotion that he didn't deserve.

"In fact," said Jenny, "I work a lot harder than he does. I do more direct care and everything. If Sean gets a promotion next month and I don't, I'm going straight to the hospice board to complain. And if Sheila gives me any flak about it, I'm filing a lawsuit."

Brenda went straight to Sheila and told her everything Jenny had said.

"Well," said Sheila, "I appreciate your coming to me with this. Now I have to decide what to do about it!" she sighed.

1. What classification of problem worker is Jenny? Why?

2. What are Sheila's options now? Should Sean be told what is going on? Why or why not?

3. If this situation continues, what kind of outcomes could you predict for the hospice?

Using Diversity as a Plus

DeShawn and his mother are having an argument—the usual one—about his hair and clothing as he is on his way out of the door for high school.

Mother: How can you stand it, DeShawn? Your pants are halfway down to your knees! Your underwear is even showing! And your hair! Why, if my brothers shaved those weird designs into their heads they'd be sent home and suspended! You look terrible!

DeShawn: Mom, you just don't get it. You want me to dress like some kind of 1970s geek. This is the style! This is who I am! You're as bad as the secretary at the high school who keeps asking me if I'm a gangster because of my clothes. Yeah, like a gangster is really going to be on student council, in drama club, and getting the grades I get! All of you are stereotyping me! You're so prejudiced! Why can't you see the real me?

You might think, by watching old black-and-white movies or old television shows, that there were only two groups of people in this country: white males in business suits and white female homemakers. Until the 1990s, white males did make up more than half of the workforce in the United States, but not anymore. The fastest growing groups entering the workforce today are ethnic minorities and women. Since the beginning of the 1990s, more than half of women with infants less than a year old are working, and the percentage rises when women have older children.[1]

Not only has the composition of the workforce been changing, but also the ethnic and racial composition of our country overall. People from all over the world are immigrating into the United States. Technology makes our world smaller by giving us instant access to the world with the flick of a television switch, and makes worldwide communication just as easy with telephones, computers, and fax machines hooking us up to the rest of the world.

For some of us, these kinds of changes are frightening. We don't know how to act around people from another country or even from a subculture in the United States. We don't understand them and may feel they don't understand us either. We may feel frustrated in our attempts to communicate with people with whom we haven't had much experience. In this chapter, we'll discuss the issue of **diversity** and how to take advantage of the strength that comes with a diversity of knowledge and life experiences.

PREJUDICE

When we talk about some of the negative feelings that exist between people of different groups, we're talking about **prejudice,** which is one type of attitude. All attitudes have three parts: what we think, what we feel, and what we do. All three are the same whether we're talking about objects, people, events, or situations. So, it doesn't matter whether we're talking about rainy weather, politics, or pizza with anchovies, the three parts of an attitude are still there. We may *think* to ourselves: "Anchovies are salty and ugly." We may then *feel* a negative reaction to anchovies: "Oh, gross! They look like fish bait, and taste like something that's been in the refrigerator for a year!" We next *do* (or choose *not* to do) something based on our thoughts and feelings. In this case, we probably will choose not to eat the pizza with anchovies.

The prejudice that is specific to attitudes about other people has

---

[1] United States Bureau of the Census, Current Population Reports (1989), and United States Bureau of Labor Statistics (1990), *United States Library of Congress,* Washington, D.C.

three components: **stereotypes,** our beliefs about people based on what group they belong to; **bias, a** feeling about people based on our beliefs; and **discrimination,** the action we take based on our thoughts and feelings.

Stereotypes

Stereotypes may be positive, negative, or neutral. They may contain a kernel of truth or they may not. Regardless, they are usually over-simplified, overgeneralized—that is, applied to all members of a particular group—and exaggerated. And because stereotypes place *all* members of a group into a category without recognizing that in-dividuals are not always the same, they have a negative effect on people.

Bias

The prejudgment of certain people based on their membership in a group or category is called bias. We all have this kind of prejudice whether we want to admit it or not. We have strong likes and dis-likes about people based on some characteristic about them, some-thing as simple as how they dress or as complex as their political or religious beliefs.

Discrimination

Discrimination can be an action, or merely the intention or inclina-tion to act. Not all stereotypes and prejudices result in discrimina-tory acts, but individual acts of discrimination usually come from stereotypes and bias.

MAJOR TYPES OF DISCRIMINATION

There are many types and targets of discrimination in our society today. The most common forms are racism, sexism, and economic prejudice.

Racism

Racism is discrimination based on a person's race or ethnicity. Even though the Civil Rights Act of 1964 made racial discrimination ille-gal, it is still a very explosive and controversial topic in this coun-

try. Other countries or regions also face this problem; the former So-
viet Union, Ireland, and the Middle East have serious conflicts
based on ethnic group membership. In the U.S. workforce, **institutional racism** can still be found. This type of discrimination may
not come directly from stereotypes or prejudice, but it still has the
effect of discriminating against people in particular groups. For example, a state police force may have a height requirement of five
feet, nine inches for officers, which may unintentionally eliminate
most women, many Asians, and many Hispanics from employment.

Sexism

Sexism is discrimination based on gender. Many of us—both male
and female—learn from an early age that women are "supposed"
to be dependent, cooperative, emotional, and undemanding. Men
are "supposed" to be strong, assertive, logical, and unemotional.
Because of these stereotypes, sexism is often found in the workplace. For example, many people believe that women do not make
good managers because of their feminine characteristics. Although
discrimination based on gender is illegal and women's average income has been rising in recent years, women are still not found at
the highest levels of management in business and government as
often as men. As a group, women often find their promotions stop
at a certain level below the promotions of men. This artificial and
invisible effect on womens' climb up the career ladder is referred to
as the "glass ceiling."

Economic Prejudice

Economic prejudice is a conflict between the "haves" and the
"have-nots." This is an ancient battle that has sparked major social
and economic upheaval such as the French Revolution of 1789, and
Russian Revolution of 1917, and the Communist takeover of Cam-
bodia in 1975. One theory about the cause of economic prejudice is
that frustration and aggression can occur when competition exists
between people. Economic prejudice between the haves and the
have-nots works both ways: The haves may see the have-nots as
lazy, worthless, stupid, and undeserving while the have-nots see
the haves as greedy and selfish.

Other Targets of Discrimination

Many targets of discrimination don't fit into the three types of discrimination just described. These include overweight people, homosexuals, the elderly, the disabled, religious groups, and pregnant women. As with sexism and racism, discrimination against people in these groups is also illegal.

SEXUAL HARASSMENT

We have been hearing a lot in recent years about sexual harassment. What is it? The Equal Employment Opportunity Commission (EEOC) defines sexual harassment as any unwelcome sexual advances, requests for sexual favors, or any other verbal or physical actions that are of a sexual nature. This would include acts such as forced fondling, sexual slurs or remarks, unwelcome flirting, sexual teasing or jokes, sexual questions, and sexually suggestive pictures. The key term to remember here is *unwelcome* sexual acts. If the people involved are not in full agreement that the behavior is wanted, then you have sexual harassment.

Company Policy

How can sexual harassment be reduced in the workplace? Whether you are a victim of harassment, a manager, or an ordinary worker, sexual harassment hurts everyone's morale. There are some ways to reduce it in a company setting.

1. **Have a policy statement written at your company.** It should be written in clear language so that everyone understands it, using large print, and it should be brief enough so that everyone will take time to read it.

2. **Make sure the policy statement is posted in a public place.** The location should be central enough so that all employees can see it.

3. **Talk about the policy.** Refer to it in memos, or talk about it in a group, so that it doesn't turn into just another memo sent out by the boss.

How to Avoid Being a Victim

As an ordinary worker, you can reduce your chances of being a victim by:

1. Asking or telling the person to stop.
2. Telling other workers what is going on.
3. Reporting the acts to your supervisor or someone in charge.

Ignoring the problem and hoping it will go away doesn't work. It will only increase your stress level. The worst response is no response.

PREJUDICE AND SELF-ESTEEM

Extremely prejudiced people are often people with low self-esteem. Tolerant people are more likely to be people who have high self-esteem. As your own self-esteem improves, keep an eye on your personal prejudices, and you may find them softening or even disappearing.

Victims of discrimination often suffer from low self-esteem, too. If you have ever felt prejudice from another person or group, you know how stressful and hurtful it can be. Being a victim of discrimination can cause us to take two basic kinds of action:

1. **Blaming ourselves.** This includes actions such as withdrawal, self-hatred, and aggression against our own group.
2. **Blaming outside causes.** This may lead to fighting back, becoming suspicious of outsiders, or showing increased pride in our own group.

One of the biggest dangers of discrimination is the tendency for it to become a **self-fulfilling prophecy**—that is, the victim starts to believe that the prejudice is true and then becomes what the stereotype claims. For example, school children who are told they are slow, stupid, or failures often become just that—and they give up trying to succeed in school.

REDUCING PREJUDICE

What can we do to reduce feelings of prejudice and acts of discrimination in the workplace? Negative ideas are often hard to get rid of, but prejudice is not inevitable! Steps taken in the workplace should include all three of the following ingredients:

1. **Increasing contact between groups.**   This will add to interaction and communication between people of different groups. Exposure to other people often leads to liking them.
2. **Equal status between groups.**   Contact by itself is not enough. If the only women you see at work are on the cleanup crew, for example, you may think that women are not able to do any other kind of work.
3. **Cooperation and interdependence.**   Cooperation, instead of competition, is a way to help people accept each other. When we have to rely on each other to meet our goals (interdependence), conflict is greatly reduced. Working together works!

Key Terms

diversity

prejudice

stereotypes

bias

discrimination

racism

institutional
  racism

sexism

economic
  prejudice

sexual harassment

self-fulfilling
  prophecy

Review Questions

1. Facing our own feelings of prejudice can be difficult, because we all tend to keep our self-esteem intact by believing that we are fair people. Consider your own feelings about different groups of people. What do you think about them? How do these thoughts make you feel? How do you act toward them?
2. Describe instances you may know of where sexual harassment occurred. What was the outcome? Is there a sexual harassment policy in place at your workplace or campus? Is it enforced?

3. Think of a situation where you were told you could or could not do something (for example, a parent told you that you were "the smart one" who always got good grades). Did a self-fulfilling prophecy occur?

4. Suppose that you are in charge of a program to reduce prejudice at your workplace. How could you increase the cooperation and interdependence there?

5. Think about groups of teenagers you know of, or groups from your own high school experience. Can you identify the stereotypes about those groups—for example, nerds, jocks, skateboarders, cowboys, or druggies? How do these beliefs make you feel? How do they make you act toward teens in those groups?

Multiple Choice

1. The fastest growing groups entering the work force today are:
   a. Teenagers and women.
   b. Women and ethnic minorities.
   c. Illegal aliens and minors.
   d. All of the above.

2. What percentage of women with children under one year old is working?
   a. Under 33 percent.
   b. 50 percent.
   c. Over 75 percent.
   d. Over 50 percent.

3. All attitudes have what three parts?
   a. Prejudice, concern, and feelings.
   b. Positive, negative, and neutral thoughts.
   c. What we think, what we feel, and what we do.
   d. Situations, decisions, and discovery.

4. Stereotypes may be:
   a. Positive.
   b. Negative.
   c. Neutral.
   d. All of the above.

5. Individual acts of discrimination usually come from:
   a. Corporations.
   b. Stereotypes and prejudiced feelings.

c. Employment situations.
d. Nonemployment situations.

A Little Harassment

Rebecca had been working for the past five years at a timber mill in the Eastern Oregon town where she grew up. It was the highest paying job in town, and it seemed that everybody either worked at the mill or left town after high school. She was in tears one Friday afternoon and about to quit her job, though, as she stumbled through the parking lot toward her car. Her supervisor, Fred, saw her and stopped her.

Fred: What's wrong, Rebecca? You look like you just lost your best friend.

Rebecca: I can't stand it anymore here, Fred, the guys tease me all day long, tell dirty jokes, and today before I left Clint threw a bucket of water on me and said he was having a wet T-shirt contest. All the guys laughed! No one even tried to stop him! They treat me like dirt!

Fred: I don't think they mean anything by it, Rebecca, I think they're just having a little fun.

Rebecca: Well, it's not fun to me, it's sexual harassment, and somebody's going to answer for it!

1. Does this qualify as sexual harassment, or is Clint just having a little fun? Use the definition of sexual harassment to decide your answer.

2. What is Fred's responsibility in this situation as Rebecca's supervisor?

3. What other steps can Rebecca take in this situation to stop Clint and the other mill workers from doing things she doesn't like?

28

Manage Your Time Wisely

Tammie and Shelley, both nurses in training, were finishing up loose ends in the hospital where they were doing their clinical training one busy Friday afternoon.

Shelley: Tammie, will you stay a little late and give me a hand updating these patient records?

Tammie: Shelley, come on! You know how busy I am! After my shift here, I still have to study for that drug dosages test on Monday, pick up my husband from work, get groceries, pick up Tara from basketball practice, get Brandon from his band rehearsal, fix dinner, and get ready for my in-laws' visit tomorrow! It seems like all I do is run around playing catch-up!

Shelley: You know, Tammie, you'd be a lot less scattered and constantly pressed for time if you were more organized. You need to manage your time better!

Tammie: That's easy for you to say! You don't have 15 different things going on at once, all the time!

Shelley: Exactly my point. With as much as you have to do every day, you can't afford to waste any time. You need to set aside some time to do some planning and get a schedule together.

Tammie: Shelley, I just don't have *time* for that!"

Sound familiar? Like the old saying that it takes money to make money, it also takes time to make time. That is, it takes time for us to plan efficient use of our time, but when we feel pressed for time, we don't like to take the time to plan out our schedules. But the only way to get off the time roller coaster, feeling like we're rushing from one crisis or job to the next, is to practice **time management.**

PROCRASTINATING

Procrastinating means putting off until later the things we should be doing now. One of the biggest problems in time management is procrastination. It is also a major way to create stress for ourselves. As we read in an earlier chapter, stress is damaging—and we're hurting ourselves by creating more stress unnecessarily. Why do we procrastinate? According to one expert, we gain some obvious benefits and some hidden benefits by procrastinating.[1] Hidden benefits include getting back at people who are demanding, hoping that someone else might get tired of waiting and do the work for us, having other people see how overwhelmed we are and thus not give us more work to do, and the special feeling we get when we're excused from working so hard, or others give us special attention for working hard.

STEPS TO STOP PROCRASTINATING

Procrastinating is an intentional choice that we make. We can also make the choice *not* to procrastinate. We all could probably use some help in reducing procrastination. Here are some steps to get started.[2]

1. Get going. Don't wait for motivation to magically come to you. Get started with whatever you are working on, and motivation will come to you. Once you start a job or a project, it doesn't take long to get on a roll to keep going at it for awhile.

2. Plan.   Whatever the job is that you must do, don't say to your-

---

[1] From David Burns, *Ten Days to Self-Esteem* (New York: Morrow, 1993).

[2] Ibid.

self that you'll get it started "one of these days." Instead, make a plan. Will you start it now? Today? What time? What parts of the job will you do today? How long will you spend today on the part that you've planned?

3. Break it down. Break big jobs down into little parts. Start with, say, 15 minutes of work on the project. Don't think that you have to do it all at once. If you look at the *whole* job instead of smaller parts, chances are you will feel too overwhelmed to get started. Start working on the smaller parts. If you finish the smaller part of the job that you have scheduled for that day, quit—without feeling guilty—or decide to go ahead and work on another part.

4. Think positively. What negative thoughts are you having about yourself that make you feel anxious? What is it that keeps you from getting started? Do you feel like a failure for not getting the project done? Are you afraid that other people will laugh at you or make fun of the work that you have done? Do you feel anxious because it might not be good enough? Replace those negative thoughts with more realistic, reasonable, and positive thoughts.

5. Reward yourself for work done along the way. Give yourself a little treat or reward when you finish those smaller parts. Don't wait for the entire project to be finished before you boost your self-esteem by, for example, patting yourself on the back, taking a walk, renting a videotape that you've been waiting to see, or relaxing in a hot bath.

6. Give yourself some credit. Don't feel like a failure for not getting the entire project done or for doing work that you feel was not good enough. Give yourself credit for the parts of the job that you did finish. Give yourself some credit for learning to manage your time wisely. And give yourself some credit for putting an end to procrastination!

USING TIME WISELY

Sometimes we plan too many things for one time slot. This is called **overloading time.** Sometimes we don't use the time that we do have. Wasting available time is called **underutilizing time.** Managing our time means using time wisely by not wasting or overloading our time.

SETTING UP SCHEDULES

We need to set up two kinds of schedules for ourselves: long-term and short-term schedules. **Short-term schedules** can be set up on a daily or a weekly calendar. **Long-term schedules** are set up on a monthly or yearly calendar, putting our long-term goals and important **target dates** into the plan. The target date is the date that a project or task is due or must be finished by. To help keep your time organized, include your family, work, and personal goals and times in the schedule.

To make your schedule work better for you, start with something fun to motivate you to keep going. Cross off items on your list after you finish them. You'll be surprised how rewarding this can be! Reward yourself with a fun task after every task you don't like.

Figure 28–1   Daily Schedule

	Urgent	Can't avoid	Important	Other
7:00 a.m.				
8:00				
9:00				
10:00				
11:00				
12:00 noon				
1:00 p.m.				
2:00				
3:00				
4:00				
5:00				
6:00				
7:00				
8:00				
9:00				

Don't try to fill up the entire schedule; you'll feel overwhelmed. You can always add more tasks later. Each day try to finish one task you've been putting off. Try to finish this before lunch. This helps you feel that you've accomplished something, which can be a boost for the rest of the day's work. These tips will help motivate you to keep your schedule going.

Short-Term Schedules

Use the daily schedule in Figure 28–1 for appointments, class times, meetings, errands, and other specific information that you need to remember on a daily basis. Make notes in the columns, so that you can remember how urgent or important each item is. Items that are noted as urgent will stand out, and you will be more likely to finish them.

In Figure 28–2, you will plan important target dates and goals on a weekly plan. This short-term plan is not as specific as the daily schedule shown in Figure 28–1.

Take a look at your daily and weekly calendars after the end of a few days and weeks. Were there many items that you didn't finish? The calendars are a good visual sign of procrastinating or over-

Figure 28–2   Weekly Schedule

Sun.	Mon.	Tues.	Wed.	Thurs.	Fri.	Sat.	Sun.
1/5	1/6	1/7	1/8	1/9	1/10	1/11	1/12
a.m.							
p.m.							

loading of your time. Make adjustments to your daily and weekly planning schedules that are more honest about how much you will be able to do (in the case of procrastination) or more realistic (in the case of time overloading).

Long-Term Schedules

In your monthly long-term schedule (see Figure 28–3), makes notes about target dates for that month. For example, you may have a project due or an important deadline that you have to meet.

In Figure 28–4, make notes about your top-, middle-, and low-priority goals for the year. These might be family and personal goals, such as filing income taxes, or losing 10 pounds by June. They should also include career goals, such as getting a presentation ready for a conference at the end of April. Make notes of the

Figure 28–3   January, 199__

	Sun.	Mon.	Tues.	Wed.	Thurs.	Fri.	Sat.
Week 1				1	2	3	4
Week 2	5	6	7	8	9	10	11
Week 3	12	13	14	15	16	17	18
Week 4	19	20	21	22	23	24	25
Week 5	26	27	28	29	30	31	

Figure 28–4   Long-term Yearly Schedule

Jan.	Feb.	Mar.	Apr.	May	June	July	Aug.	Sept.	Oct.	Nov.	Dec.
Top											
Mid											
Low											

specific goals you would like to reach each month. Keep this schedule in sight, so that you can remind yourself about the goals you are aiming for. From time to time, you will need to revise your yearly schedule to account for new goals, new target dates, or old goals that you may decide to drop.

As with the short-term schedules, take a look at how well you reach your goals and stay on schedule over time. You will need to adjust these long-term schedules, too, to make up for procrastination and overloading or underutilizing your time.

 ## Key Terms

time management	short-term schedules	target dates
overloading time		
underutilizing time	long-term schedules	

Review Questions

1. Why is time management important?
2. What is procrastination? Why does it hurt us?
3. What are some steps we can take to reduce procrastination?
4. What kinds of tasks or goals should we include in short-term and long-term scheduling?
5. What is meant by overloading and underutilizing time?

Multiple Choice

1. Underutilization of time can be defined as:
   a. Trying to fit too many activities into one time slot.
   b. Not making good use of the time we have available.
   c. Putting off things we must do until a later date.
   d. Setting goals for things we want to get done.
2. Which of the following is *not* a suggested way to reduce procrastination:
   a. Put together small pieces of a project into one large task before starting.
   b. Reward yourself for work done along the way.
   c. Reduce negative thoughts.
   d. Get started on the task without waiting for motivation to happen.
3. A suggestion to help your schedule planning work would include:
   a. Start with something unpleasant to get going.
   b. List as many tasks as you can think of.
   c. Do fun tasks first, followed by unpleasant tasks.
   d. Cross off tasks as soon as you've finished them.
4. One of the reasons why we procrastinate is:
   a. We don't know how to do the task.
   b. We are lazy.
   c. We are overwhelmed with too many things to do.
   d. Other people might see we have too much to do and then not give us any more work to do.
5. Procrastination and poor time management can lead to:
   a. Stress.
   b. More free time for fun activities.

c. Lowered anxiety.
  d. Better health.

Off to School, or Not?

Jamilla is a 40-year-old homemaker. Now that her two children are in school full time, she is thinking about going back to college to finish her degree in botany. Her husband agrees that going back to school is a good idea for Jamilla. He wants to help more with the housework and the kids so that she can do it, but he travels about two weeks a month for his job. Their kids are active year-round with chorus, Scouts, soccer, and the regular social activities of an eighth-grade boy and a fourth-grade girl.

Jamilla is pretty sure that she can handle the academic work. She picked up a registration packet in September. Now it's January, and she still hasn't turned in the registration and financial aid information, or made it across town to the college for her required advisory appointment.

Maybe this is all a big mistake, she thinks to herself. I'm just too old. I blew my chance at college, now I just have to deal with it.

1. What kind of scheduling does Jamilla need to consider right now, short term or long term?

2. Set up a sample yearly schedule for Jamilla. What kinds of things does she need to include in her plan?

3. Is Jamilla procrastinating in getting started at college? If you think she is, what specific steps should she take to overcome this?

29

Set Some Real Goals for Your Future

Jody and Lita were talking about Lita's 20-year-old son, Malcolm, at work one day. Malcolm had lost his college baseball scholarship the year before because of a knee injury, but during his time off from college he had landed a great job. It wasn't in his field, but it paid more than most of his college graduate buddies were making, and the benefits were good.

Jody: You know, Lita, it seems like Malcolm always lands on his feet, no matter what. He just kind of floats through life, without a care in the world. And he seems so happy—even when things don't quite go his way!

Lita: I know he may look like he's floating through life, but I'd say it's more like muddling through. Malcolm has no idea what he wants out of life. When I ask him what his plans are for his future, he can't even tell me what he wants to be doing next week! He's really un-happy! I wish he'd just set some goals for himself, and then start working toward them!

SELF-DIRECTION AND SETTING GOALS

In an earlier chapter, we talked about motivation, or what gets us going. We know from studies in psychology that the strongest kind of motivation comes from within ourselves. People who are self-motivated, or motivated by **intrinsic rewards** (internal rewards) are also probably self-directed. **Self-direction** means being able to set short-term and long-term goals for ourselves.

The more specific the goals are that we set, the more clear they are, and the better they work to motivate us. **Short-term goals** are specific action plans for things you want to accomplish right now, or put on your calendar for the immediate future. These can include, for example, finishing a project at work, or taking a college course. **Long-term goals** are those things you decide to work toward as part of a life plan for the future. These could include finishing an accounting degree and getting a job in accounting, or eventually getting an advanced degree in your field, or becoming a better parent. Short-term and long-term goals are both important to your success. Breaking long-term goals down into several manageable short-term goals is a way to be successful in the long run.

MAKING A LIFE MISSION STATEMENT

Figuring out what our goals are is probably not a common activity for most of us, but **goal setting** is really a fairly simple process. Mostly it's a matter of just taking the time to do it. Start with long-term goals, asking major questions such as, "What do I really want to do with my life?" or "What do I want my life to have meant after I'm gone?" or "What is it that I want to get out of life?" Your answers to these questions can help you develop a **life mission statement,** or long-term goals for your life. All of your short-term goals, then, will be directly related to your life mission statement.

If your life mission is to help other people, for example, choose short-term goals that allow you to achieve your life mission over the long term. If you see yourself helping others in the health care field but you've always worked in a hotel, set some short-term goals that let you try out the health care field and see if it is really what you want to do with your life. Volunteer your time at a hospital or hospice. Prepare meals for the disabled or deliver meals to elderly shut-ins. Take some classes at a local college. Talk to people who are working at the job that you see yourself doing.

Analyze Your Strengths and Weaknesses

Take a realistic look at yourself and decide how you are doing at managing your goals. Strengths and weaknesses fall into several different areas. Answer the following questions to touch on several areas of possible strengths and weaknesses.

1. **Do you know yourself?** What are your top three life goals? What needs are most important to you? Do you reward yourself for attaining a short-term goal? How?

2. **Do you work on your goals?** Do you prepare yourself before working on goals? Do you have daily routines for each major goal? Do you set realistic goals for yourself?

3. **Do you manage your time well?** Do you try not to procrastinate? Do you have good work habits? Do you regularly try to reduce your stress level?

4. **Are you good to yourself?** Do you use positive statements when you talk to yourself? when you talk to others? Do you take care of your overall health?

5. **Are you organized?** Do you plan or schedule each day on paper? Are your home and work spaces organized? Can you find what you need when you need it?

6. **Do you have support for your goals?** Do your friends and family members support your goals? Do the people you work with support your goals? Do you feel that you are getting what you want out of your life?

Think about the answers to these questions. If most of your answers are no, then it is time to work on setting and managing goals for yourself. Try to change your regular way of doing things so that the answers to the questions above are mostly yes instead of no.

Fear and Failure

Fear may stop you from carrying out your plans and working toward your goals. To fight your fears, you must first identify them.

Imposter phenomenon.   One of the most common fears that is a barrier to reaching long-term goals is called the **impostor phenomenon.** People who suffer from this fear are usually successful, but they are afraid that they did not achieve that success as a result of their own talents and hard work. This is the fear of being found out as imposters, that they have gotten away with something they shouldn't have. They are afraid that they are not smart enough, not good enough, or not hard working enough to keep on succeeding. This fear holds people back from achieving goals.

Fear of failure.   Two other kinds of fear that can hold us back are fear of failure and fear of success. **Fear of failure** happens when we are afraid that we are going to look bad to those who are judging us. People who have extreme fear of failure may quit trying and give up. They stop trying to achieve both short-term and long-term goals.

Fear of success.   Life experiences usually cause the **fear of success.** People with fear of success have not had much success in their lives, and they start believing that they don't deserve to have any. They may feel that they will not live up to their reputation if they do succeed at something. They may feel uncomfortable after a success because the feeling is so unfamiliar, and they don't like it. This may lead them to stop setting and trying to meet short-term and long-term goals.

How can we eliminate these fears, once we have identified them? One way is to practice emotions that are the opposite, such as courage and self-confidence. It is physically impossible to feel two opposite emotions at the same time. Try it! Some people, though, may have fears powerful enough, so that they need to go to a counselor for help in eliminating them.

Find Your Niche

In biology, a **niche** is any place where a human or other living creature can best survive. To be successful in setting and meeting our goals throughout our lives, we need to find out where we can survive and thrive and feel content. We can think of this as finding our niche.

Families of skills.   Part of understanding ourselves and finding our niche comes from figuring out what our skills and talents are. Job-hunting expert Richard Bolles describes three **families of skills:** those that use information, those that involve people, and those that use objects. Skills with information include gathering or creating data, managing or computing data, and storing or using it. Skills in working with people include helping others, instructing, caring for people, exchanging information with others, coaching or giving advice, persuading, entertaining, or supervising others. Skills in working with objects include skills with the body (such as athletics), using materials (such as arts and crafts), using tools or machinery, building or constructing, growing plants, or caring for animals.[1]

We can figure out what our skills are by listing the kinds of things we are good at and like doing, or do the most often in our spare time, and deciding what family of skills these fit into. Take some time to list your skills and talents. The following list of categories should help in this process.

1. **Health and physical stamina.**   Are you healthier than the average person your age? Do you enjoy physical activity?

2. **Quantitative ability and interest.**   Are you good with numbers? Do you like working with numbers?

3. **People skills.**   Do you get along well with others? Do you like spending time with a variety of people?

4. **Leadership skills.**   Do other people see you as a leader? Do you find yourself taking charge?

5. **Mechanical ability.**   Do you like fixing equipment, maintaining it, and learning how it works?

6. **Musical ability.**   Do you pick up a tune easily? Do you like to sing or play a musical instrument?

7. **Artistic ability.**   Do you like to draw, paint, or do other kinds of art? Do you think you could do those things, if you tried?

8. **Creativity and discernment.**   Can you see opportunities

---

[1] Richard Bolles, *The Three Boxes of Life and How to Get Out of Them: An Introduction to Life/Work Planning* (Berkeley, CA: Ten Speed Press, 1978), pp. 167–94.

where other people don't? Do you find creative solutions to problems?

9. **Self-assurance.** Do you have the self-confidence to believe that your ideas will work, even when other people are doubtful?

10. **Speaking and writing ability.** Can you express yourself effectively? Can you speak to a group without being nervous?

You are very likely to have talents in one or more of the areas on the list. You can probably think of other areas of ability to add to this. The next step is to apply those skills to a specific goal. Check out library books on different careers, talk to people in different occupations, and try new hobbies. Don't feel limited by what others have done. Taking some risks and constructing your own niche can lead you into new and exciting directions.

Key Terms

intrinsic rewards

self-direction

short-term goals

long-term goals

goal setting

life mission
    statement

imposter
    phenomenon

fear of failure

fear of success

niche

families of skills

Review Questions

1. Have you ever found yourself being reluctant or afraid to tackle a new job because you might fail at it? Describe the situation. How could you explain this, in terms of the material in this chapter?

2. Thinking about the three families of skills described by Richard Bolles, are you working at a job that matches your skills and your interests?

3. What are your immediate short-term goals? Are your short-term goals helping you work toward your long-term goals?

4. Why is it important to develop a life mission statement? Do you have one? Describe it.

5. Would you say that you have found your niche? If so, how did you decide that it truly was your niche? If not, what would it take for you to find your niche?

Multiple Choice

1. When a human or other living creature has found the place where it will survive the best, we say it has found its:
   a. Niche.
   b. Interests.
   c. Abilities.
   d. Talents.

2. Susan's idea of a relaxing evening while she is away at college is to work on the bonus questions for her statistics class. She would best fit Bolles' ____ family of skills.
   a. Information.
   b. Tools.
   c. People.
   d. Social.

3. Deciding what you want to do with the rest of your life and setting goals to get there can help you develop your:
   a. Short-term goals.
   b. Self-direction.
   c. Life mission statement.
   d. Time-management plan.

4. People who have not had much success in their lives and don't believe they deserve any success may develop:
   a. Fear of success.
   b. Fear of failure.
   c. Fear of impostors.
   d. Impostor phenomenon.

5. Knowing your strengths and weaknesses, working on your goals, managing your time, and being organized are some steps you can take in:
   a. Analyzing your strengths and weaknesses to help manage your goals.
   b. Finding your niche.
   c. Finding out which family of skills you fit in with best.
   d. Reducing fear of failure.

Emma the Imposter

Emma had just finished a two-year business degree at the local community college. She was looking forward to the graduation ceremony in just a few days, which would make the whole thing seem more real. Several businesses in the area were offering interviews for graduates at the campus placement center, and Emma had signed up for them all. Emma's first interview was with a large advertising agency in town. The interviewer introduced himself, and Emma introduced herself. They were both smiling and nodding pleasantly, but Emma was panicking inside. Her thoughts were racing, as she thought to herself, What am I doing here? I should never have signed up for this interview! I'm not ready for this kind of job! It's too much responsibility! I can't handle it! I don't know how I even passed all these business courses—my professors must have just felt sorry for me or something! I'm not that smart! What if they hire me and find out how stupid I really am? I'm not good enough to do this job! This is so humiliating! I should never have gone to college! Emma realized that the interviewer had asked his first question. "I'm sorry," she said politely, "could you repeat that?"

1. Why is Emma thinking those thoughts to herself? What is she afraid of?

2. How can Emma reduce these feelings for her next interview?

3. If you were Emma, would you have signed up for every interview offered? What advice would you give Emma in choosing what jobs to interview for?

Index